HO[W TO LIST]
AND SELL
RESIDENTIAL
REAL ESTATE
SUCCESSFULLY

BARB SCHWARZ

SOUTH-WESTERN

THOMSON LEARNING

Australia · Canada · Mexico · Singapore · Spain · United Kingdom · United States

How to List and Sell Residential Real Estate Successfully
by
Barb Schwarz

Printed in the United States of America
    5 6 7 8   06 05

For more information contact South-Western/Thomson Learning, 5191
Natorp Boulevard, Mason, Ohio, 45040. Or you can visit our Internet site
at http://www.swcollege.com

For permission to use material from this text or product contact us by
• **telephone: 1-800-730-2214**
• **fax: 1-800-730-2215**
• **web: http://www.thomsonrights.com**

ISBN

0-324-13965-9

I lovingly dedicate this book to my husband, Kirk, for his everlasting love and dedication to me and my/our work. I dreamed this program would be used by a company one day. Little did I know that instead of a company it would be the entire country. We have accomplished this together, program after program, city after city, across the country. Without him this would not have been possible.

I also dedicate this book to the agents, brokers, managers, and owners who are using my program with its ideas, techniques, and tools in their own marketplace to serve sellers for the betterment of the seller, the company where they work, their own careers and lives, and for the betterment of our profession.

Contents

Preface ix

1

The Beginning 1

2

"Let Me Tell You How I Work" 9

Time Up Front Versus Trouble Later On 11
Three Steps to Listing Real Estate Successfully 12
Professional Policies 15

3

Step 1: Meeting Sellers for the First Time 20

Rapport Building with Sellers 21
Sellers' Motivation Is Key to Control 29

4

The Career Book®: Key to Your Credibility 31

Credibility 32
Creation of Your Own *Career Book* 35
Getting Started 36

Simple but Crucial Procedure 42
Guaranteed Success 45

5

Prospecting and Uses of the Career Book® 46

Source 1: Sellers 48
Source 2: Buyers 48
Source 3: For Sale by Owners 49
Source 4: Open Houses 52
Source 5: Builders 53
Source 6: Anyone! 54

6

Step 2: The Detailed Report 58

Setting the Stage for Presentation 59
Control of Flow 62
Language 63
Practice Makes Perfect—and Increases Income! 64
Parts of the Presentation 65

7

The Marketing Portfolio™ 68

Marketing Portfolio 69
Start with Your Company 71
Listing Process 71
Educate Future Sellers about Staging Homes 71
Professional Information Sheets for Sellers 73
Separate Marketing Booklets about Every Listing 73
Teach How the Multiple Works 74
Ways Brokers' Open Houses Work 75
Quality Flyers 75
Top-Selling Agent List 75
Company Advertisements 78
Relocation 79
Best Idea for Sustaining Communication with Sellers 81
Forms That Are Used in the Sale and Closing 82
Education of Sellers Today! 83

8

Part One of Your Detailed Report: Exclusive Marketing Program 85

Education! Education! 86
Presentation of Exclusive Marketing Program 88
Exclusive Marketing Program 90
Secrets of My Success 96
Ending of Marketing Presentation 104
Master Your Marketing Program 106

9

Power Behind the Secrets of My Success 107

Secrets of Successful Marketing 108
Synergy! 119

10

Part Two of the Detailed Report: Comparative Market Analysis 120

Understanding Equals Cooperation 121
Building Your Comparative Market Analysis 12
Staged Homes 127
Laying the Groundwork 128

11

Recipe for a Sale: Pricing the Property Right 129

Setting the List Price: Ingredients of a Sale 130
Pricing Triangle 133
Controllable Versus Uncontrollable Ingredients 135
The Right Price 136
Bottom Line 137
Refusal of a Listing 140
Listing Agreement 141

12

Step 3: Listing the Property 143

Careful Approach 144
Attention to Details 144
Review Listing Agreement 145
Sellers' Listing Packet 146

13

Staging™ the Property: The Inside Story 149

Conquest of Fear 150
Great Idea: The Car Story 152
Three C's of Staging: Clean, Clutter, and Color 152
The Key: Do It Now! 157
Tips for Selling 159

14

Staging™ the Property: The Outside Story 170

Power of First Impressions 171
The Buyers' Point of View 171
Tips on Selling for Outside of Property 174
Tips for Showing a HOme 178
Work Equals More Money—for Your Sellers and You! 181
The Difference Staging Makes 182

15

Ways to Ensure that Sellers Finish Preparing Their Home for Sale 183

The List! 184
Getting Commitment to Finish List and Pack Up Piles 184
Quality Appearance 190

16

Organization and Success 191

Success by Getting Your Act Together! 192
Three Areas to Organize 192
Two-Box System 195
Organization Is the Name of the Game 196
Time Management 196
Gold Mine 199

17

Your Journey of Success 200

Development of a Plan 201
Steps for Reaching Goals 201
Courage to Try! 204
One Last Look 205
Use All of the Marketing Techniques 208
Success! 208

Appendix 211

Barb's Favorite Sayings—Words that Work 212
Barb's Favorite Stories—Words that Work 214
Tips for Selling 216
Recipe for a Sale 218
Pricing Your Home 220
Barb's Marketing Update Report 224
Barb's Tools for Success 227
Steps to Make Your Loan Application Easier 228
Glossary of Financing Terms 230
Your Personal Moving Check List 232
Amortization Chart 235
Estimate of Purchaser's Expenses 236
Career Book Introductory Letter 237

Preface

I have written this book for you. Whether you have been in real estate for ten years or ten days, times have changed and the business of listing and selling real estate has changed. Service is more important than ever. Service, to me, is the total name of the game.

This is a proven program of service. It works. It has been put to use and tested by over 100,000 real estate agents across the country in every state in the union.

It is a detailed program that brings success. Successful agents are successful because they have a program that they follow and constantly use. Most of the agents who drop out of the business did not have or did not follow a program.

You will see that this whole program is based entirely on service. Yet, you are the key. You are the key to providing the service, and that service will lead you to your own success. If you put this program to work, you can literally double your income and have more fun at the same time.

I am going to put you to work. I believe that in real estate too many of us are not prepared. Even after being in the business for several years, too often agents are simply not prepared for what sellers expect and demand today. Therefore, I am going to ask you to become better prepared than ever before. This is going to mean taking some time to explore some new ideas and build new tools that will serve you repeatedly for years to come.

Before we begin, I also have another reason for writing this book. That is to help raise the image and reputation of the real estate industry. It is time that we raise the level of professionalism in real estate. As we do this we will also raise our reputation in the public's eye. They go hand in hand. One cannot happen without the other. Together, I know that we can do this. Any agent using this program will immediately help achieve this goal because of the service on which this program is built. It won't be easy, but agent by agent, we can impact the industry in totally positive ways. I am going to ask you to set new policies, new standards of excellence, that will lead to more success than you have ever had before. Now, let's get busy!

1

The Beginning

Do you want to make more money in real estate? I can hear your answer—a resounding "Yes!" That's good, because you are looking in the right place. This book can help you make a lot more money than you are now making. You will make more money—even by the time you finish reading the last chapter of this book—if you will trust the ideas and techniques that I will share with you and apply them to your own career.

These techniques work, if you do. And it does take work. There is no other way. It takes rolling up your sleeves, digging into projects, digging into builders' inventories, digging into resales, doing the marketing, and getting properties sold. My complete philosophy is to serve the seller—first, last, and always! If you do that then the money will follow in all the commissions you will earn.

Believe me, in the world of real estate, listing is where the action is. I love the relationship I have built with my sellers. I have their names on the dotted line. I have a commitment from them. And I have a commitment to them.

Now, a lot of real estate salespeople in the real estate industry are doing things the same way they have always done them. For years, agents have walked into properties, looked around and said, "Well, gosh, I think you can get about $98,000 for this home. I'm sure I can sell it. Sign here, and I'll put an ad in the Sunday paper." The sign goes in the yard, the ad shows up in the Sunday paper, and that's what they call marketing. Those days must come to an end.

When I got into this business about eleven years ago, I saw a real lack of service. I saw that a lot of people did little to market properties they had listed. Unfortunately a lot of agents in this business still continue to approach real estate that way. But the true professionals in real estate know that the secret to success in our business is to serve the seller—first, last, and always.

Did you know that as an industry we don't have a very good reputation? In a recent survey conducted by George Gallup, Jr., and reported in the Los Angeles Times, people were asked how they viewed the honesty and ethical standards of those in various careers. The results of the survey indicated that out of twenty-five occupations across the country, we, as real estate agents, rated in the bottom five. As far as the public is concerned, when it comes to honesty and ethics, we rank right down there with used car and insurance salespeople! That's not too encouraging, is it? You and I don't belong in the bottom five, but it is up to us to change it. I believe a lack of service has cultivated that poor reputation. So, the best way to wipe out that poor image is to give sellers and buyers more service than ever. Plus, let me ask you something. Do you work long hours in this business? Of course you do! Do the sellers you represent know everything you do for them? Why not? Because many times we don't tell them. It is my strong contention, throughout this book, that we need to educate our sellers as to how we work and what we do for them. The key is to tell them up front.

You and I, together, can build and shape our profession as real estate agents, by serving our sellers in a more professional manner. This effort will ultimately result in an improved public perception of our industry, not to mention an increased income for you personally.

Good service will give you an edge. I believe good service is the difference between a good agent and a mediocre one, a successful agent and a struggling one. If you want to be ahead of the game, serve your sellers professionally and efficiently. I have developed a simple but comprehensive three-step program that can help you do just that. It starts with service when you first meet your potential sellers and goes all the way until the sale closes. Sellers deserve that.

Don't be afraid to take control! To be able to serve your sellers to the best of your ability, you have to have control of the situation, in much the same way you have to let your doctor have control over you if he or she is going to be able to help you when you are sick. Now, when I talk about control, I'm not talking about a mean or rude type of control. That's not what I mean at all. Control doesn't need to be a negative word. Control simply means managing the situation. As a real estate professional, you can't do your best job if you don't have control. Control means working to price the property right, **Staging**™[1] the home to sell, and directing the marketing process so the sale will go smoothly and quickly to bring the best price possible for your seller. That is why people hire us!

Control is necessary, but many of us lack it when we work with prospective sellers. We are afraid to control, mainly because

[1]Staging™ and Stage™ are trademarks of Barb Schwarz. All rights reserved.

we fear it will cost us the listing we want. We assume our potential sellers will react negatively and that we might lose a listing because of it. I know. I learned all this the hard way.

Experience is the best teacher. There is a reason for everything I'm going to share with you in this book. Those reasons have come from mistakes— failures, if you will— that I have made. Actually, I don't really believe there is any such thing as a "failure." Rather, I have learned from the mistakes I have made, so I call them "experiences." I have worked hard to correct my mistakes and to put what I have learned from them to work in my business. Some of the experiences I am going to share with you come from the times I didn't do so well. I would say to myself, "I'm not going to let that happen again. I fell flat on my face in front of that seller. I didn't know what to say to him when he asked me that question. I didn't know how to handle him when he raised that objection. Next time I'm going to think of a way to take care of that situation ahead of time so I won't have to go through that same experience again." In sharing this information with you, I want to save you from those poor experiences. I am going to show you the ideas and techniques that I have developed during a long period. They are ideas that work, ideas that can save you a lot of learning time, and they can definitely make you more money!

This book will teach you ways you can list with control and make more money by

1. Handling objections before they come up. You see, if we head off the objection before it comes up, we're not going to have an objection. If we put that seller's mind to rest before the objections ever come up, then we are not going to have to deal with any objections!

2. Developing your own **Career Book**®2 and **Marketing Portfolio**™.3 These tools are priceless when it comes to creating credibility, educating your seller, and answering objections long before they are expressed.

2*Career Book*® is a federal registered trademark of Barb Schwarz. All rights reserved.

3*Marketing Portfolio*™ is a trademark of Barb Schwarz. All rights reserved.

3. Sharing many of my phrases or sayings that are absolutely dynamite in defusing objections before they come up.
4. Getting the seller to prepare the home for the market, which I call "*Staging.*" This can be a tough one for agents. You know, as I tell my sellers, a lot of agents don't know what to tell sellers in order to get their property ready to sell. Sometimes they are afraid to tell sellers what to do with the property to get it ready to sell. They don't want to hurt the sellers' feelings. It is my contention that when I list a property, it is my job to say, "Here is what we need to do, Mr. and Mrs. Seller, to get your property ready to sell." We are talking about marketing an important product, probably the most important product in that couple's life—the family home. They are looking to us for guidance as to how to do it. I strongly believe that teaching the seller how to **Stage**™ the property should always be part of that guidance. Remember, even used car dealers *Stage* their merchandise. The key is to teach the sellers why this process is important ahead of time, and then when we have their commitment we teach them how to do it. Don't worry, by the time you finish this book you will know how to *Stage* a property inside and out!
5. Pricing the property correctly. A property that looks attractive also has to be priced right. If it is priced too high for the price range of the neighborhood, it doesn't matter how good it looks. We have to have price and condition working in balance. So, I have come up with some definite techniques and tools that will help you get that property priced right.
6. Marketing the property to get it sold! We can go through all the other goals, but if we don't do the marketing we should do, we won't get it sold. This book gives you a total marketing package, combining the strength of many marketing techniques.

Now, before we go on I would like to tell you a little about my background so that you know a little more about me. After all, we are going to have a special relationship as you read my book, and I think it is important that you know a little bit about where I came from and my background.

After I graduated from high school in Kansas, which is where I grew up, my family moved to Seattle, Washington. I earned a degree in education and music from the University of Washington, and went on to teach in the Bellevue, Washington, public school system. What does all that have to do with real estate and listing residential property? More than you might think. Even though we don't usually associate teaching with real estate, a lot of the techniques and ideas that I am going to share with you in this book I adapted from skills I developed during my teaching days. When I left teaching, I ran my own interior design business. My minor in college was design. For about five years I worked with single-family homeowners, helping them design and decorate their homes. I also worked with builders and owners of commercial and multi-family housing. When we get to the section in this book on ways to improve the condition of a property, please don't say, "Well, Barb can do that because she has a design background." Actually, the things I am going to share with you have nothing to do with design. They are just common sense and basic ideas to create more space and less clutter so that purchasers can mentally move into a potential home when they first see it.

After several years in design, the wonderful world of real estate came along. One day I happened to call on a real estate broker for another reason, and he said to me, "Why aren't you in real estate?" All I could say to him was, "Gosh, I love homes. I used to hold open houses for builders in Kansas when I was in high school. I don't know where the agents were, but I was the only one holding the houses open. I've thought about getting into real estate but I've never done anything about it." He looked me square in the eye and said, "It sounds to me like you are procrastinating." When he said that it hit me like the proverbial ton of bricks! I headed out the door and I didn't look back. I applied for my license, passed the test, started in this fantastic business, and have loved it ever since.

During my first eighteen months in real estate— and this may shock you— I didn't get one of my listings sold. Not one! All the listings I had were overpriced and did not look very good. After a while I started to realize that the real money makers in the business were listing agents; and if I were to become successful in the listing game I had to come up with a better way to get my listings priced right and *Staged* to come on the market. I also really enjoyed working with sellers. I decided one of the reasons I enjoyed working with them was that they put their names on the dotted line. They made commitments to me, and they made them in writing. I knew if I worked hard, they were going to stick with me, and I, for sure, was going to stick with them!

Now, you may say to yourself, "This woman couldn't sell her own listings...how does she plan to tell me how to list property?" If you remember what I said earlier, you are going to benefit from some of the mistakes I made. And I made a lot of mistakes in that first year and a half. I spent a lot of time hitting my head against the wall and saying to myself, "There's got to be a better way." What I am telling you is that I developed this program "in the streets" working with sellers. No matter what happened— or didn't happen— I was responsible to my sellers. I thought, "Hey, Barb, you haven't been very honest with these people. You didn't lie to them, but you also didn't tell them the truth. You didn't tell them how you thought their property should *really* be priced when it came on the market. You didn't tell them what you thought they should do to prepare their house for sale.... You didn't want to hurt their feelings.... You were afraid you wouldn't get the listing." Does any of this sound familiar to you? So, I made a commitment to myself, to my sellers, and to all the people who would be my future sellers, which I have stuck by all these years. This commitment is— no matter what— I am going to tell all my sellers the truth. We need to be honest. We need to tell them the truth. As I say to my sellers, "There are agents out there who will tell you what they think you want to hear, and I really believe in sharing the truth that you deserve to know."

You don't have to take a listing. If the sellers make it impossible for you to find a buyer it will only frustrate you and your sellers. No matter what, don't be afraid to be honest with your sellers. They will appreciate your honesty when you point out to them that you are being honest for their own sake.

So, I started to be truly honest with people. Guess what happened? I started to get my listings priced right, *Staged*, and sold! My sellers started to get their equities. Each time I came up with even more effective techniques!

These same techniques are going to make you more money, and they are going to make real estate more enjoyable for you. Everything you learn in this book you can apply to your own business. People come up to me during my seminars and tell me how easily they have been able to work my program into their own careers. They say to me, "It works!" And it can work for you too.

I want you to enjoy this book. But there is something else I would really like for you to do. I am going to ask you to make some commitments. I want you to take some risks. I want you to keep an open mind. When you first come across some of the ideas I am going to share with you, you might say, "Wait a minute, Barb. I don't know if I can do that." I want you to promise something right now. Promise me, and promise yourself. Say, "OK, I'm willing to give this a try." Do the things you are afraid to do. That's when you really start to grow. When you take the step that is a little bit scary to take, you open yourself to new and wonderful experiences. Sometimes, at the very least, you learn what not to do.

Be willing to try! Now let's get to work.

2

"Let Me Tell You How I Work"

In this chapter you will learn

1. What the "Let me tell you how I work" approach is and how to use it.
2. How to use this philosophy to help find prospects.
3. Control = Education and Education will give you Control!
4. My exclusive listing program and overview of the service that I give to all of my sellers!
5. How and why to develop your own Professional Policies.

People often ask me, "Barb, where do you find business? Where do you go to find prospects and the people who want to sell?" Well, the answer to that is easy. Prospects are everywhere! With the right approach, prospects will find *you*. They will practically fall out of the trees and hit you on the head if you know how to shake the branches a little.

I have a special technique for finding prospects everywhere I go. I call it the "Let me tell you how I work" approach. It is as simple as it sounds, and it works! You just tell people who you are, what you do, and how you do it. It is amazing how few people actually know what real estate agents do. Because most agents don't tell clients what they do, it is even more important for you to learn and use the program I'm about to give you. You must let people know who you are, what you do, and how you and your service are so much different from all the rest. Remember, the public put all of us, as real estate salespeople, in the bottom five. By educating people about who you are and what you do, you open yourself up to an almost endless source of prospects. By taking just a few minutes to give them an overview of your service, people say, "Wow, you do all that?" They will tell other people about you, and they will remember you when they are ready to sell their homes. Tell them up front, "Let me tell you how I work."

I actually use that exact phrase when I am on a floor call, meeting someone in an open house, or meeting anyone, anywhere, at any time. If you don't share with your future clients up front how you work, all their assumptions about you will be based on the experience they had with the last agent they worked with, and that may not have been a good experience. Don't take the chance of letting your reputation be based on that encounter.

Most of us as real estate agents introduce ourselves by saying our name and the name of our company. Such as, "Hello, my name is Barb Schwarz, and I work for Barb Schwarz Real Estate." From now on please don't stop there. Instead, say your name, the name of your company, and follow that immediately with, "Let me tell you how I work." Then give them a quick oral outline of the service you'll be performing for them.

TIME UP FRONT VERSUS TROUBLE LATER ON

Some agents actually believe it is a waste of time to educate sellers up front as they list homes. Spending more time with your sellers initially can save you a lot of problems later. This time gives you the opportunity to educate your sellers about how you work, and why it is important that they trust you as a professional. This is crucial to getting the right price set and for *Staging* the home later. By getting to know your sellers and letting them get to know you, you determine if they are motivated to sell and if you can work together as a team. Many benefits will show up both early and later if you will spend more time up front with the sellers.

I firmly believe that educating the seller will give you control. Remember I've proved it by learning the hard way. In any relationship one of the parties usually needs to have control to make the relationship work. This is true in a doctor-patient relationship, accountant-client relationship, and real estate agent–seller relationship as well. If you remember this phrase it will help you with all aspects of your career. Actually I want you to memorize one of my favorite sayings:

Education = Control and Control = Education.

I'm talking about educating your sellers and doing it up front! If later on in the listing process you have trouble getting the sellers to price the property right or getting them to *Stage* the home, either you have sellers who really don't want to sell, or you didn't educate the sellers enough up front.

The easiest way to gain professional control is by telling buyers and sellers how you work. "Let me tell you how I work" is the key, I believe, to do that in a brief professional way. You can say it in any number of ways that are comfortable for you such as: "I'd like to take a minute to explain how I list and sell homes," or "I work differently from a lot of other real estate agents— let me briefly explain all of the services that I provide all my sellers." You can say it many different ways, but "Let me tell you how I work" puts you ahead of most other agents because you took the time to educate your sellers. Education equals control, and control will give you more power to help more sellers. It works! Try it!

I make two separate visits with my sellers as I list their homes. Now, you may be saying, "Two visits as you list their property! Are you kidding?" From my experience, it takes two visits (and in certain instances even three) to get the job done and to do it right. You see, there can be a lot of problems later if we go there only once, walk through the house, cross our arms and say, "You have a nice home. I can get it sold. I think we can get, oh, $245,000 for your home. I'll put an ad in the paper. Sign here." How can you make a judgment by just seeing a house one time and then giving the sellers a price? I don't care how hot your market might be, things change very quickly. It is difficult to be an expert in every block in every area in your city. This quick-list approach also does not give enough time to educate your sellers properly about pricing, *Staging*, or marketing.

Now remember, many of the points I am teaching are based on experiences from the beginning of my career, which did not go well. When I first started listing homes, I tried to crowd everything into one visit. But I wasn't pricing each property correctly. I wasn't putting the property in proper showing condition. I was not educating the sellers and letting them know how I worked. And I also had a lot of problems. I soon discovered that one of the best ways to avoid those problems was to visit each of my sellers at least two times. I spend a lot of time up front with my sellers. The more time you spend with them in the beginning, the fewer problems you will have down the road. I strongly recommend that for any agent. Invest the time in the beginning, and you will not have to spend a lot of time later solving problems or explaining why or what you are doing.

THREE STEPS TO LISTING REAL ESTATE SUCCESSFULLY

The three steps of service in listing a property are presented in Figure 2-1. A discussion of each step follows.

Listing of Property: Three Steps of Service

"Let Me Tell You How I Work"

Step 1	Step 2	Step 3
• Meet the sellers • Have the sellers show you their property • Explain your three steps of service; repeat "Let me tell you how I work" • Leave your **Career Book°** with the sellers	**Present your Listing Presentation** *(the Detailed Report)* • Outline your Exclusive Marketing Program *(Use your **Marketing Portfolio™** when presenting your marketing program to your future sellers.)* • Explain the Comparative Market Analysis for your future sellers	• Complete the paperwork to bring the sellers' home on the market *And with their permission:* • **Stage™** their home by making suggestions, room by room, inside and out, to prepare the home for sale

FIGURE 2-1 Listing of Property: Three Steps of Service

Step 1

Step 1 is for you to meet the sellers and to see the property. You need to see what kind of property you will be selling. You'll need to check comparables for that area, after you see the home, and before you return for Step 2. You have to check condition and location as well. Just as important, you have to see if you want to work with the sellers. Do they really want to sell? This is very important! If they aren't motivated to sell don't continue to spend time with them. Step 1 is also an important time for you to build rapport. Remember, all sellers are really looking for a salesperson who they can like and trust, so spend time to build your credibility with them. You'll want to leave your *Career Book* (discussed later in Chapter 4) so that the sellers will find out all about you! This will help to build the like and trust relationship for you, in a way that nothing else can.

Step 2

Step 2 is for your listing presentation, which I call the Detailed Report. Think about the words "listing presentation." To me they almost sound like kindergarten words. You know what? Those words, which we have used in the industry for years, landed us in the bottom five. I have received greater respect from sellers over the years by using the words "Detailed Report" when I refer to the presentation I have prepared for them. Many of the sellers we sit down with have to prepare reports for their employers, and they seem to appreciate us more if we refer to our presentation as a report.

After you have met the sellers and seen their property, you have to put together a detailed two-part report. Part 1 describes ways you are going to market and sell that property. Part 2 is your pricing analysis. I will explain both aspects of the Detailed Report in greater depth later in this book.

Step 3

Step 3, then, is actually doing the paper work to list the property, filling out the listing agreement, and then going through the property with the sellers to make suggestions about what to do to bring it on the market. This means to go room by room with the sellers inside and then outside to make recommendations of things to do to prepare the property for sale. *Staging* the home is crucial! In a slow market it can help the property sell quicker. In a fast market, *Staging* the house can help it sell for even more money. That means more commission for you. *Stage* your listings! It's where the money is. (As the person who has taught *"Staging"* to the real estate industry, I will explain *Staging* in greater detail later in this book.)

So, you can see each step has a valid reason. Sometimes agents will say to me, "Barb, can't you combine steps two and three?" Well, of course you can. If your sellers are ready to sign on the dotted line, and you are ready to go to work together... list the property of course! But it takes time to do it right. So spend the necessary time to do it right if you do combine the two steps. *Staging* could be the same day as visit two, the next day, or (in a few cases) even six months later. But presenting a professional detailed report like the one I will outline for you in later chapters takes time, and so in most cases I recommend that you need to come back another day to do the paper work or *Stage* the house.

Service is the name of the game. It always has been, and I truly believe it always will be. It is what you want when you go to your favorite department store or when you take your car in for repairs. If you do not get service you will start to shop somewhere else, won't you? Sellers are the same. They want and expect service, and if they don't get it they will list with someone else. So, no matter how many trips or visits or steps you take to list a home, remember that service is the key. You can take the results to the bank.

I really believe in certain guidelines concerning this three-step program. Does the company you work for have certain guidelines or policies? Of course they do. Do they usually break them? I assume the answer is no. I believe that as individual real estate salespeople we should have our own unbreakable guidelines as well. These are not meant to conflict with the policies of your company. They are to give you added strength as the professional you are.

PROFESSIONAL POLICIES

Say these two words out loud right now: "Professional policies." I want you to develop policies of your own, detailing how you will and will not work. Then, I want you to stick to them. I owe it to you to explain some of my professional policies concerning the three-step program I have shared with you. They do give extra strength to the program and to me as a sales professional. You can decide if and how you will adapt them to your career.

Some of my professional policies follow.

Policies for Step 1

It is one of my policies never to see a property without at least one seller there to show it to me. No one knows the property like the sellers, and I might miss something if I just looked at it by myself. Another reason for this policy is this: Not only do I want the sellers to show it to me, but I also want to show it to the sellers. Let me explain. You know when you see the property for the first time you see things that the sellers do not because they have lived there for so long. You and I see the property like a buyer will, and we need to point some of these things out to the sellers. An example might be, "Oh, Mr. Seller, tell me about that." This is as we see a big spot on the ceiling, for example. Many times the seller will look up, take a step back, and say, "Gosh, I didn't even know that was there." If the sellers had not been there to show you the house so you could also show it to them, you would not have been able to do this. Not only does this get the sellers to start to think how important *Staging* their home will be, but I find it is easier to bring back a realistic suggested list price and have them accept it. Make it a policy to have at least one seller at the property the first time you see it.

There is one exception, but not really. That is when the house is vacant, and the sellers live out of town. If this is true, take pictures, slides, or even a video and send it to them pointing out things that need to be done. Do this before you ever present your listing presentation, the Detailed Report. Otherwise, all sellers think they live in an irreplaceable castle. Again it helps, ahead of time, for them to start to think about preparing their home for sale, and they will usually be more realistic about the price.

Remember, if the sellers tell you on the phone that they both work, the key is under the doormat, and they suggest you go look at the house by yourself, you want to inform them of the following in a nice way. "Mr. Seller, I understand what you are saying, however no one knows your home like you do, and I have made this one of my 'professional policies' to have one of you there to show your home to me." Stick to your policies. They work for you, and they work for your sellers.

Policies for Step 2

One of my strongest policies, which I have never broken, is the following. When I give a listing presentation, I want both of the sellers present. If you sit down with just one of the owners, the other owner cannot know what you do and can sabotage your efforts. You may not get the listing. How do you educate someone who isn't there? You can't do it. I can't do it. No one can do it. If three people from a bank are on a committee and will pick the listing agent to list the house, please do not sit down with just one member because the other committee members will not know what you do.

If you arrive at the sellers' home, and the wife informs you her husband just called to say he'd be late and to go ahead and give your presentation to her, what are you going to say? Acknowledge that he was trying to save you time, but that you have made it a "professional policy" of yours to sit down with both of them as owners. "It is just too important, so let's reschedule," tell her. And then reschedule. It works. Remember, doctors have policies, and if they break them the patient could die. Accountants have policies, and if they break them the accountant could actually go to jail. We should have professional policies as well. So make yours and stick to them.

What if you are working with a family and the husband, let's say, has already moved to the new city to start working? I suggest giving the report to the wife in person and sending another original to the husband. Set a time to call him on the phone to go over it in detail; that way they are both educated about your marketing program and about the pricing. If you don't do that then the wife knows the program and the husband doesn't. The husband is in another city wondering what in the world you are doing to sell his house. This is because he wasn't educated, and without that education he will usually get out of control.

> **Remember, Control = Education.**

When you give your presentations please take time in doing so. No one can educate a seller in fifteen minutes. It takes time! Spend time up front and you won't have to spend time answering objections from the sellers down the road. Anyone who is only giving sellers fifteen-minute marketing presentations today is not doing the job. Why? Because marketing today means more that just putting in an ad and putting up the sign in the front yard. My presentations run, on the average, one and a half to two hours. I hope yours do, too. Sellers love being educated, and it is another reason you'll get the listing— because you took the time.

One more policy of mine regarding my presentations is to always give marketing to the sellers before you give pricing. If you present the pricing portion of your report first, their brains are on only one thing— the price. They will never hear your marketing plan for their home. Present the marketing part of your report first, and tell them that because they will be paying you for marketing and selling their home, they owe it to themselves to know everything up front. They do care. They will listen. Then after that, and only after that, go on to the pricing of the home. Make it a policy and stick to it.

Policies for Step 3

I learned this policy the hard way. Do not *Stage* a home until you have the sellers' names on the dotted line. Why should you *Stage* someone's home and have them sell it For Sale by Owner or list with someone else? I know, because I made this mistake, once. Once was enough. I had called on a For Sale by Owner and as we were looking through her home I said, "I know some things we could do right now that might help you sell your home." I was thinking this might impress her and help me secure the listing on their home. Remember, I had just met her, and I hadn't even presented my marketing or pricing presentation. She was eager to hear and learn everything I had to share so I spent about two hours with her making changes throughout the home. About six o'clock she informed me they were going to have dinner guests at seven and could I come back the next day with my report. I said, "Well..., of course." I came back the next day, and they had actually sold the house overnight to the people who had come to dinner. Do you know who those people were? They were their very best friends. They said, "We've been in your home many times, but it has never looked so good. We'll buy it. It has more room than we realized." I learned the hard way. Never *Stage* a home until a signature is on the bottom line. *Staging* is extra power and strength you bring to your sellers. Let's not give them that power until they give us their commitment in writing. This is one of my policies, and I hope you will make it yours as well. I tell my sellers that *Staging* their home with them is an extra additional service that comes along with me, at no extra cost. This can help them get the most amount of equity in the shortest amount of time.

By the way, something great did come out of the bad experience I had with that For Sale by Owner. It is one of my best sayings, and I hope you'll learn it. It is part of what I share with sellers when we actually do *Stage* their home to make sure that they will do it and keep it looking good.

> **Buyers only know what they see, not the way it's going to be.**

That saying works! It works when sellers aren't sure if they should replace the carpet. It works for rooms that need painting. You see, out of every unpleasant experience there is so much we can learn. I would probably have not developed that saying if I had not had that unpleasant experience and seen, firsthand, that even best friends can't imagine what a house will look like after it's *Staged.*

Policies work. They are so important. They will help you have more fun in this business. They will help you to be better organized. And, when a seller tries to throw you up against the wall (figuratively speaking, of course) policies can help you help the seller understand. Sellers have policies in their line of work as well. Don't think they don't. They can't break them, because if they did, they probably would find themselves out of a job or career. Share your policies with your sellers. Ask for their respect for your policies, which benefit them as well. Let them know: "This is the way I work."

3

Step 1: Meeting Sellers for the First Time

In this chapter you will learn

1. How to build rapport with your sellers.
2. The four key things you should be doing as you go through the property.
3. A detailed explanation of what to do and the objectives to have the first time you meet the sellers at their home (step 1).

RAPPORT BUILDING WITH SELLERS

When you go to meet the sellers and view their home the first time, try to arrive just a little bit early. As you drive into the neighborhood, you should really be looking around the block. You have to spot things. Look for the homes that look terrific. Look for the homes that have problems. You want to see where your sellers' house is in relation to all this. Is it next to the house that has a boat, a recreational vehicle, and six motorcycles parked in the front yard and weeds up to the windows? If it is, that is going to hurt the sellers' property when it goes on the market. Or is it sitting between two spotless, wonderful-looking homes? That makes a difference.

So, as you drive to the potential sellers' home, really look around the entire block. When you approach the sellers' property, pull up across the street. Don't pull into the driveway, right up to the garage door. You want to get the purchaser's view. Many of the top showing agents park purchasers across the street so they can get a good look at the property. So, just sit there a minute and look at the property. Take notes. Use a notepad to make two lists— one for the things you like about the house, and the other for things you would like the sellers to change when you list the house. On the "like" list, you might put "freshly painted, good color." (There's nothing worse than coming on a freshly painted house that is the wrong color.) Also, you might list "lovely rose garden in front yard." Beautiful! On the "change" side, you might list that "shrubbery is overgrown." Other problems might be that "front door needs painting and shutter on second story is hanging loose and coming down." You'll have to get the sellers to take care of all these things when you list the house. Now pull into the driveway, shut off your car and go up to the front door. Be sure you have your scratch pad, *Career Book*, and possibly your briefcase with you.

From the first time the sellers open the door until you say good-bye, you want to work on building rapport with your potential clients. You can gain a real edge on the competition by showing sincere interest in the sellers and their property. Enthusiasm for the sellers' property is irreplaceable. At the front door get your hand right out there and make contact with the sellers. When you shake hands be sure you have a nice, firm grip. Not too loose and not too tight. There is nothing worse than shaking hands with a "dead fish" or shaking hands with what I call "the killer crunch." You should have your *Career Book* with you (as you will learn in the next chapter) and possibly your briefcase as well. Once on the inside, ask the sellers if you can set your things down. Set them on a soft surface such as the sofa or on the carpeted floor. Never set them down on an end table or coffee table, as you could scratch the furniture with your briefcase or purse. Scratch the furniture, and you probably won't get the listing.

Now I'm going to let you in on a wonderful secret that really works! As soon I have met the sellers and put down my things, I keep my eyes open for something very important— the pets. I hope you're smiling. I know a lot of people laugh when I say this, but I have made thousands and thousands of dollars from the dogs! When you go to see the sellers' property, haven't you noticed that if they have a dog (or cat) they always introduce us? If the sellers have a dog, I reach right into my pocket and pull out...did you guess it? A dog biscuit. Now, I always ask the sellers, first, if I can give the dog the biscuit. They always say yes. Don't you dare give the dog a biscuit without asking, because if the dog choked (and croaked) you wouldn't get the listing.

You know the saying: "Love me, love my dog." I can't tell you how many times I have gone to visit sellers who had a pet, and was able to list his or her property because I paid attention to the animal. I also know how important this is because sellers sometimes tell me about other agents who didn't get the listing because they weren't nice to the pets.

Let me go back in time and tell you how dog biscuits came into my listing career in the first place. One day, in the beginning of my career, I was supposed to show a successful businessman a high-priced property. I went to preview the property ahead of time, by myself. I pulled into the driveway and started to get out of my car. All of a sudden a large Doberman pinscher lunged at me, growling and snarling, with the biggest set of teeth I'd ever seen up close. I immediately jumped back into my car. I sat there shaking while he proceeded to jump at my window barking and growling with slobber streaming down my window. I tried rolling down the window just a little bit to baby talk with him, which was the only thing I could think of at the time. That didn't work. I quickly rolled the window back up and tried to think. "I've got to see this house. No one seems to be home. What am I going to do?" All of a sudden it came to me. Go to the grocery store, buy dog treats and come back and bribe him. I drove to the store, got the dog biscuits, came back to the house, and "killer" was still there. I rolled down the window just a little, threw out the first biscuit to the dog and said, "Please eat this bone." It worked! So I threw out another one. He ate that one, too. I then opened the car door just a little, and stuck out one of my legs. It was still attached. So, holding the box of biscuits in my hand, I headed toward the front door throwing one right after another until I unlocked the front door and jumped inside. After I saw the house, I went back out front, and now the dog was sitting there wagging his tail, waiting for me, and licking his chops for another treat. I still had the box in my hand, of course, so I threw biscuits all the way back to my car until I was safe inside and then drove away from the house. Later I put the box of biscuits in my trunk and promptly forgot about them.

One day I was sitting at the office working floor time. You may call this "up time" in your office. A call came in from a woman. She was very formal on the phone, and I worked hard to get an appointment to see her. I wanted that appointment because she had a large home in the most exclusive area in town. I got the appointment. When I went to see her for the first time, I'll never forget the fact that she never smiled as we went through her home together. Not once did she smile. Her name was Karla, and she was very stiff and formal as she showed me the property. We went through her home together, and she pointed at each room calling it by name, and that is all she would say. "Barbara, this is the kitchen. This is the living room. This is our master bedroom." I was thinking to myself, "I'm not getting anywhere with this potential seller." Then, as we went into the guest room, I noticed the dust ruffle on the bed started to move. I said, "Karla, what's under the bed? Why is the dust ruffle moving like that?" Speaking in her stiffly accented voice, she said, "Oh, Barbara, that is my little dog, Fufu." I said, "Oh, I love dogs, I really do. Can I talk to him?" She said, "Oh, Barbara, he's hiding under there because he's afraid of you, and he will not talk to strangers." (Notice she called me a stranger as a real estate agent.) I said, "Would you mind if I try? I really do love dogs." She said, "Be my guest. But it won't do any good. He won't talk to you." By this time I was thinking, "What have I got to lose?" So, I got down on my hands and knees, raised the dust ruffle, and said, "Hi, Fufu! How are you doing in there?" The dog, a little white poodle, just sat there, panted, and shook. Then I remembered I had the dog biscuits in the trunk of my car. I said, "Karla, I'll be right back." And I went to get the dog biscuits. When I came back and Karla saw the box she smiled for the very first time. She said in her own stiff way, "Oh, Barbara, that is very sweet, but he will not take that from you. He will not come to anyone but me." So, I asked, "Well, would you mind if I try?" She answered curtly, "Oh, I suppose you can try, be my guest, but it won't do any good." I got back down on my hands and knees, raised the bedspread and said, "Fufu, look here! Barb has this little bone for you. Would you come out and see me? Would you come out and say hi?" Guess what happened? Not only did the little dog come out— shaking all the way— but he actually started to eat the biscuit! Do you know what happened next?

Karla stood up straight, looked me square in the eye and said, "You shall list my home!" I said, "Karla, I don't understand. You haven't even seen my presentation yet." She looked at me and said, "Anybody my little dog Fufu trusts, I trust. You shall list my house."

I made $5,000 off of one dog bone because I listed her home and it sold in two weeks, full price. Now you know why I say that I've made thousands of dollars from the dogs! Since that time, I've carried dog biscuits with me wherever I go. Never underestimate the pets that any seller has. They can help take you to the bank! Pets are sellers, too!

The other thing I look for as soon I'm in the house is children. Let's do the same thing with the kids. No, I don't mean give them dog bones. But do treat them with respect. You know, a lot of agents don't pay any attention to the kids, and I think they are making a big mistake. Children are sellers, too! I've seen a little kid come up and say, "Daddy, that man that was here was mean. I didn't like him." Do you think that man will get the listing? No way. I've heard little girls or boys say, "Mommy, that lady that was here before was rude," and for that reason, the agent was not called back and didn't get the listing. When you talk to those small children, squat down on your knees. Get down at their level so you face them eye to eye. Having giants walking around you all the time isn't any fun. Talk with them about their rooms and their toys, anything of interest to them. The kids can be fans of yours and really help get you the listing. Try it. It works.

Throughout your first visit, continue to build rapport, even while you are accomplishing your other objectives. I always recommend that you do four other important points the first time you meet the sellers at their home.

1. Make compliments in every room in the house. Just pick out the things you like, as an agent, and compliment them. This is easy to do and very natural. Try to compliment something about the house, but if the house is plain then compliment some possession of the sellers. This also works.

2. Get used to using the words, "seller-and-agent team." You will find that saying these words to the sellers several times during your first visit in their home will have a positive effect. They start to think of you as their agent and part of their team.

3. Mentally *Stage* their home. This is really important. You don't want to have to figure out later on what you are going to ask the sellers to put away or do. As you go through each room in the house, I know you recognize what needs to be put away or done when you see it. If there are stacks of magazines on the floor, you know it. If there is not one ash tray but four of them, you know it. If the sellers have too many collections, you know it. Never tell the sellers all of the things you are thinking about at this point, as it is too soon in the educational process, and you don't want to hurt their feelings or offend them when you have just met. But it is very important to *Stage* the house mentally the first time you see it. I also know when I return for Step 2 with the sellers, I am going to suggest a list price that reflects the home's value after being *Staged.*

4. If the sellers have collections, make a big deal of them. This is not only fun, but there are several important reasons why you need to do this. When the sellers have a collection in their home it is because they love it. If you draw attention to it and praise it, you are showing an interest in the sellers that will help in building rapport. That is the first reason to draw attention to the collection. But there is a double win

here because when you have actually listed the house and the sellers' names are on the dotted line, you can refer back to the first time you saw their collection. By sharing the following analogy with the sellers you can get them to put it away entirely.

"Mr. and Mrs. Seller, do you remember the first time we met how I was so attracted to your collection of (whatever the collection is). Well, I am thinking we had better pack it up and put it away, because if you leave it out I'm afraid the buyers coming through your home will do what I did. And that is to buy your things instead of your house. We're not selling your things, we're selling your house. You had better pack them up and put them away." This works every time, but you must pay a lot of attention to the collection the first time you go to their home, or it may not work.

To illustrate the four important things to do the first time you see the sellers, stated earlier, I will put them into a sample conversation to point out each idea.

I have just gone into the living room with the sellers and I (1) make a compliment about the large beautiful bay window. "Mr. and Mrs. Seller, I love your bay window. Look at all of the light it lets into the room and the spacious feeling it adds to your living room. Let me make a note of that, because as we work together as a (2) 'seller-and-agent team' that will really help me market and sell your home." (Mentally I am thinking yes the window is wonderful, but they have so many plants stuck in the window you can hardly see the window. When I list this home I'm going to get them to move every one of them, but I don't say anything about the plants to the sellers at this point.) Instead I (3) mentally Stage the house. We go into the den, and the sellers have a collection of stuffed ducks all over the den walls. There are a lot of stuffed ducks. I praise the ducks. "Mr. Seller, I love your ducks. Where do you shoot all of them? Have you named any of them? You have! Oh I really love this one. What is his name? Can I touch him? Oh, he is so beautiful. I always wanted my own stuffed duck." Praising the collection of ducks will make it so much easier to get the sellers to put them away after I have listed the house.

I would continue through the entire house with the sellers using this technique in every room. Practice this method, and you will find these techniques really work with sellers.

Ask the sellers to take you through every single room including the basement. Then ask them to show you around outside. (The only exception to this rule would be if your seller is 105 years old, and it is pouring rain outside.) To prepare a report for Step 2 without having walked around the exterior of that property would, in my mind, be a big mistake. You could miss big problems out there that would affect the pricing of the home. So, never prepare the report for visit two until you have gone through that entire property both inside and outside.

If you have time and weather permits, I suggest you even ask the sellers to walk across the street with you. When you go over there, you might ask, "When was the last time you stood here and looked back at your home like a buyer?" The sellers will answer, "Gosh, not since the day I bought it." This is really the truth for almost every seller. Some will actually say "never." Then ask the sellers to "think like a buyer" and tell you what they see. Doing this puts things into perspective for them, encouraging them to see the house from the purchaser's viewpoint. Turn to the sellers and say, "What do you see?" He might say, "Gee, I didn't know the roof had so many pine needles on it. Well, I can see we're going to have to get those cleaned off." She may also say, "I can't even see the left side of my house. All those bushes have grown way over the eaves. The front door doesn't look too good either."

When you've taken the sellers across the street, they are now seeing it the way the potential purchaser sees it, and that can make a big difference. This also makes a positive impression with the sellers that you are someone extra special. Probably no other agent took them across the street, and it really sticks in their minds that you were the guiding expert who asked them to think like a buyer. This also lets the sellers see their property the way it really is. They get to be the "tough guy" on themselves. I don't mention anything or point out anything until they have mentioned all the things they see. Then I will bring up anything that they didn't see that I saw when sitting across the street in my car. Taking your future sellers across the street also helps you bring back a suggested list price that they can accept more easily. Because now they have seen it from a different vantage point than from their own living room.

After you have looked over the entire inside and outside of the house with the sellers and you have taken them across the street, ask them to go back inside with you and sit down and visit for a few minutes. As you sit with the sellers back in the house, I suggest before you leave that you do a repeat of "Let me tell you how I work." (Do this whether you've already told them on the phone, in person, or not.) Telling them how you work does two things: first, you educate your sellers; second, you sell yourself.

I hope you have already told them on the phone about how you work, but it is really important to repeat it now. Give them just an overview of the work you will be doing, but not all of the details. Leave the marketing and pricing to your Detailed Report when you return.

Remember, by telling your sellers how you work, you are establishing control. If your sellers know what to expect of you from the beginning, they will be much less likely to resist your suggestions further down the road.

For example, if you wait until after the sellers have signed the listing to say, "Oh, by the way, I want to go through your house with you and tell you all the things that we need to change, fix or clean," you could run into problems. Sellers don't like surprises. So, tell them this the first time you meet them: "I feel it is my job to help you get the best price for your home. And one way I can help you do that is to help you prepare your home for sale, which I call *Staging*. A *Staged* home usually can sell quicker and for even more money in certain markets." Not only will they want you to do it, expect you to do it, but they might fire you later if you don't do it because you taught them up front why it is so important. So, you see, in the first meeting you are not only selling yourself and establishing rapport, but you are starting to educate your potential sellers about how you work. This approach is crucial for acquiring and maintaining professional control.

Before you leave, set that appointment to return and present your Detailed Report. This could be a day later or a week later. It depends entirely on your schedule and your sellers' schedules. Of course, you want to return as soon as possible. Set that time.

Now, here is where your magical tool called the *Career Book* starts to work for you. Before you leave, always explain to your future sellers that you are actually the one who will be doing the work for them, and you think it is important that they know something about you. Tell them you have put something special together about your career in real estate. Your *Career Book* shows them your background, your credentials in the business, what you did before you got into real estate, and even some of the homes you've sold for others— perhaps people in their own neighborhood. Leave the book, and let it do the talking and bragging about you. Never show the book to them. This is because it means more when they discover your assets for themselves. If you tried to show the book at this point you'd end up cheating yourself; you would never take as much time as they would on their own. I'll go into complete detail about the *Career Book* in the next chapter.

There is something else you should also be thinking about, which brings me to my last point.

**Qualify the potential sellers:
Are they motivated to sell?**

I know you are saying, "I've heard of qualifying buyers. But qualify a seller?" I have a philosophy about just taking any listing. There are a lot of sellers out there. Sometimes we take a listing just because it's there. We think if we don't take it, someone else will. Well, if you have the time, and that's the way you feel, then go ahead and take it. But listing the home of sellers who just want to experiment or "test" the market can be a waste of your time. The last thing you need is a bunch of overpriced properties and sellers who are not at all motivated. All that does is wear you down and lead to a lot of frustration. Now, I'm not talking about the house that is a little bit overpriced that you go ahead and list. I'm talking about the houses that are out of sight. You get the feeling from the sellers that they really do not want to sell. They are just not realistic or motivated.

SELLERS' MOTIVATION IS KEY TO CONTROL

When you meet potential sellers, the first thing you want to determine is their motivation. Asking questions is the best way to determine how motivated your sellers are. Don't stop asking questions until that sale down the road is closed. Their answers to those questions are going to tell you a lot. If they answer, "Well, we're not really sure. We just want to see if we can move," you might not put them high on your priority list. (When you are listing ten, fifteen, twenty-five or forty homes, you should put your sellers in a certain order of priority.) But, if they answer, "John is being transferred across the country at the end of the year. So, we have to move, and we can't afford to keep two houses," then you know they need to sell their house. They are very motivated.

When you come across sellers who do not want to let you do what you need to do to be effective, and that little voice inside says, "I don't think these are sellers I should be working for," let it go. You'll be glad you did. Don't burden yourself with it, and don't burden your company with it. Because as soon as you sign up those impossible sellers, along comes Mr. and Mrs. Ready-To-Sell, who will listen to you, give you authority, and let you have the control you need to do your best for them.

Inevitably, (and I hope you are smiling as you read this because we've all experienced it) if we take both listings, guess which seller is going to be on the phone calling every day? You walk into your office and your secretary says every day, "Guess who called?" You know it is going to be the sellers whose house is way overpriced, in poor condition, and in a bad location. They are the ones who are going to take your valuable time.

So, take time in that first visit to get to know the people and the property. What you learn about the sellers and the property in the first visit will help you in the second visit as you give your listing presentation, the Detailed Report. Spend time up front with your potential sellers. If you do that, you are not going to have the problems that could come later.

> **Remember, Education = Control and "Let me tell you how I work!"**

These points, together with your *Career Book* will get you off to the right start. And that you can take to the bank.

4

The Career Book®: Key to Your Credibility

In this chapter you will learn

1. Exactly what the *Career Book* is and how it was developed.
2. How the *Career Book* will give you more credibility than you've ever had before, regardless of your experience in real estate.
3. How you can build your own *Career Book*.

Proving to a potential client that you are the right agent to list his or her home is the first step in getting that listing. The *Career Book* is one of the most powerful tools for doing just that.

CREDIBILITY

The greatest challenge you face in listing property is establishing credibility, and convincing a homeowner that you are the person to list and sell his or her home. In this chapter, I want to tell you about an exciting tool I've created and developed called the *Career Book*. I can honestly tell you, the *Career Book* works! It is literally revolutionizing the way people list real estate all over America, because it helps build credibility for you. If I could, right now, I would hold the *Career Book* right up in front of you and say: "The *Career Book* could make you $25,000 to $50,000 more in income this year." Those numbers are really impressive, aren't they? Just think about it. If you could earn $25,000 to $50,000 more in income, wouldn't that make building your own *Career Book* worthwhile? It really can happen for you! I've seen agents all over the country boost their income by at least that much— the very first year— using this exciting tool.

Birth of a Bright Idea

As I began my career in real estate, I was virtually unknown. No one knew who Barb Schwarz was in real estate or what I could do as I set about listing residential properties. I observed that sellers had little information to guide them in making decisions about who they would hire to be their real estate salesperson. When sellers look for an agent to list the property, they often look in the yellow pages or ask a friend for help and advice. It can be just a matter of luck to find the right agent. If the sellers do not care for the agent who comes to see them, they don't call the manager of that company and say, "I didn't like Mary. Do you have another one down there you could send me?" They do not do that. They call the competition.

I started to think seriously about how little time we have to make the right impression the first time we go to see potential sellers. Maybe we make the right impression and maybe we don't. People are judgmental. Maybe they like our appearance and maybe they don't. They make judgments based on how we handle ourselves in about 30 minutes of time, not really knowing anything at all about us except what they see. And people buy people.

But how then can they decide if I'm the right agent based on just what they see? If I brag, they will think I have a big head and not hire me for that reason.

What do I have that could let them know about me? The answer became the *Career Book.*

I now want to ask you five questions, and I want you to be really honest with yourself about the answers.

1. Who does the work in representing a listing and marketing the property—you or your company? That's right, it's you! Your company knows that.

2. Who does the seller really pick? You or the company? Right again. It is you. Now, managers, I don't want to lose you here. The company's job is to find the best agents it can for that very reason. But if the sellers don't like an agent for one reason or another, you know that they call the competition. In most cases the agent makes the reputation for the company in the minds of the sellers.

3. Now, does your company have credibility? Yes! That's one of the main reasons you are with them. Remember, your company does a lot of marketing and spends a lot of money to build that credibility. Usually, companies do a great job of marketing the company as a whole.

4. Do you have credibility? Yes, you do! Of course, you do!

And the biggest question of all! Be honest with yourself.

5. Do the sellers you go to see usually know as much about your credibility as they do about your company's? The answer is no!

Let's summarize. You are the one who does the work. You are the one that the seller really picks. Your company has credibility. You have credibility. But then, notice that when you go to see the sellers they usually do not know as much about your credibility as they do about your company's. Yet we expect them to pick us when they don't know much about us. This is a little like Russian roulette. No, thank you. You can't afford to leave it just to chance. Now, think about what we take with us when we go to see the potential sellers. Most of us take our business card and a company brochure. The company has done a great job of marketing already because they appreciate the need. They understand and realize the need for marketing information about the company. But what about us? Oh yes, we have our card. It may even say GRI, CRS, or CRB on it. That is wonderful, but sellers don't know what that means. Most sellers never even bother to ask what it means. I also have my million dollar sticker on my card, but they do not know how I earned it. It is time as individual real estate agents that we also get into marketing ourselves, in addition to what our company already does. This is the age of marketing. Are you in public relations? Are you in sales? And are you in real estate? The answers are all obvious. If you don't sell yourself, then who will?

No one, that's who.

As I continued my thought process, I asked myself, "Who is my employer in real estate?" In listing property it is the seller every time. Well, if I went out to look for a new employer other than in real estate today, what would I take with me? I would have to prepare a résumé and take it with me everywhere I went. A résumé helps an employer make decisions about who he or she is going to hire. In real estate, I realized that my real employer is the seller. That's who is paying me. So, I decided to apply this idea and take it a little bit further than just a résumé. I went to the store and bought a notebook and clear plastic sheet protectors. In addition to my résumé I asked myself what else could I put in it? I went back to my office and sat down at my desk. As I looked up on my walls I saw my five company awards. I saw the clock hours I had taken in the business and the certificates that I had framed and put on the wall. I asked myself, as I want you to ask yourself, "What are those doing on your walls? Whoever sees your walls anyway?" I'll tell you who— the fellow associate agents you work with— and they are not paying you! I took my certificates off the walls and put them in my *Career Book*. I took pictures of the plaques, blew them up to 8 × 10 and then put them in my book. I put in other information about myself: my background, work record, education, and so forth. I also decided to put in pictures of the homes I had listed and sold during my career in real estate.

I started leaving my book with every seller I met, whether the contact came from a phone call, a referral, or doorknocking. Guess what happened? When I started leaving my *Career Book* with sellers, I started to get more listings. My listings sold and my income started climbing. "I've really struck gold!" I thought. And you can, too.

CREATION OF YOUR OWN CAREER BOOK

By preparing a real estate *Career Book*, you are way ahead of most other salespeople. With your *Career Book*, sellers now have something positive by which to judge you. Remember, we said people are judgmental. But now, they can make rational decisions. And most of those decisions, I find, are positive. With a *Career Book*, your image will soar! Try to imagine yourself as a skyscraper, because your image goes up about that high. You will stand out from the rest. Most salespeople either haven't heard of the idea or are just too lazy to put one together. Even if it were a perfect world and every real estate agent had a *Career Book*, please remember competition is good! It's good for you and for me, and it's really good for that seller. If the people who were competing for listings all had their own *Career Books*, it would help make the decision for each seller so much easier. No longer would the sellers throw a dart at the biggest ad in town. Please don't get me wrong, there is nothing wrong with having the biggest ad. But the sellers have the right to find the person who meets their needs the best. The *Career Book* really helps to make that happen. Besides I truly have never left my *Career Book* and had another agent leave his or hers at the same time. Even if it did you wouldn't go to a job interview in another industry looking for a job and say, "Well, I don't think I'll take my résumé because everyone else will be bringing one, too." You would say, "I'd better bring mine because others *will be* bringing theirs." Think about it. It makes sense.

Before I start to take you through my *Career Book*, there are two concepts I need to discuss. These concepts are powerful, and you have heard them all of your life. They are the reasons you like your friends and they like you. As agents we need to have them with the sellers because they can literally give us the listing. The *Career Book* shows these concepts off like nothing else can. They are the concepts of "common ground" and "credibility." Common ground can take you to the bank over and over again. There is no way that sellers can tell by looking at you that the two (or three) of you probably share common ground. There is definitely more to you than meets the eye.

Where did you grow up? Do you know how many listings I have personally gotten because my *Career Book* shows I was born and raised in Kansas? If the prospective sellers used to live in Kansas and they see I used to live in Kansas, we have "common ground." Never, I mean *never* underestimate the true power of common ground. It works. Most of us have something in common with other people we meet that would help us earn their trust. Some of these things are not immediately obvious, and that is where judgment comes into play. People tend to screen us out rather than in, based solely on what they see. People only know what they see, usually. You cannot get your background, all the accomplishments you may have in real estate, all of your credentials, and the other areas of common ground all on your business card. It's impossible. This is why the *Career Book* works so well. It helps you establish common ground as nothing else can.

The other word I mentioned was "credibility." I have talked about credibility and how the public ranks real estate agents in the bottom five of twenty-five professions. People think we are not as honest as other professionals. They think we lack ethical standards. Many times sellers know the credibility and reputation of the company that you work for, but they do not know about your individual credibility. They cannot tell that by looking at you either. No sellers will list their property with a person that they do not like and trust. Your *Career Book* will help you bridge the credibility gap by showing off your professionalism. The *Career Book* definitely helps you establish the common ground and credibility you need to help you get more listings.

GETTING STARTED

The first step you take toward building your *Career Book* is to mark a date on the calendar and write, "I'm going to put my

Career Book together." Then, pick a drawer in your desk and start collecting items that can go in your *Career Book*. When the day comes for you to put your book together, you'll have the time and the materials to do it! There is no perfect real estate *Career Book*. The size of it does not matter. It's what is inside that counts. If you are new to real estate, you can develop just as good a *Career Book* for yourself as a person who has been in the industry for ten years.

Let me share with you in detail the ideas and information that I think you should put in the *Career Book*.[1]

Ideas and Information to Include in the *Career Book*

Photos, Certificates, and Awards. Right away, you are going to be selling you. That is the key. You want to impress the sellers right away with who you are and what you have been doing. The beginning is the perfect place for you to include such things as your announcement of when you started working for the company, your background, and your résumé. If you just started working for the company recently, it is also important to include what else you have been doing. Remember, sellers have backgrounds too. You may really strike common ground in this area with them. Most people don't get into real estate as their first job out of school. The other jobs that you have had can help build credibility and common ground and that can help "sell" you to your potential sellers. If you used to be a top salesperson for a Fortune 500 company, that will give you credibility. If you used to be a US Marine, you will build rapport with those who are or have been in the military. If you used to be a teacher, that can build credibility or common ground too. You never know what in your background can create a favorable impression with the many buyers and sellers you will meet in this wonderful business. So don't be afraid to include lots of information about yourself. Whatever you are comfortable sharing will be a benefit.

In your résumé, talk about your background in depth. List any schools you have attended and extra courses you have taken. When you have secured those extra clock hours, where does that certificate go? If it goes in your drawer, it is not working

---

[1]To order the *Career Book*, please refer to the Appendix of this book for complete details.

for you. If you put it up on the wall, very few people will come to your desk to see it. You now know where it should go— right inside your *Career Book* where sellers can see any and all certificates you have earned. Whether your certificates were for accomplishments in real estate or a former career, put them in the book.

Awards are crucial. They can definitely take you to the bank. Take your awards to your future employers so they can see what you've done. Just take pictures of every single one of them, whether they are real estate related or not, and put them in your *Career Book*. You don't have to brag at all because the sellers will see them in your book. In other words, the book does the bragging for you.

Don't forget anything about your background. Screen yourself in, not out! The smallest item may be just the thing that strikes a familiar chord of common ground with your potential sellers. Be proud of your background. If you are not proud of yourself no one else will be either. This is really a brag book. So brag. People love finding out and reading about someone else. And now that is you.

Be sure to include photos in your *Career Book*. If you were ever in the newspaper, put in the articles. Show off the personal side of your life. Put in pictures of your family. People love seeing your family. That can be spouse, children, parents, even brothers, sisters, or close friends. Yes, that may sound corny at first, but corn can make you rich! You should even put in photos of your pets. Remember my dog bone story. Sellers have pets, don't they? And they love their pets. Some sellers seem to love their pets more than their kids so show off your pets, and they'll take you to the bank as well.

Show off your hobbies. Golfers love to talk to golfers. Fishermen love to talk to fishermen. Skiers love to talk to skiers. Common ground in these areas can really break down the walls and get you more listings.

Letters of Recommendation. As you work with people, ask for letters of recommendation from them. If you don't ask, they may not write you one. You can do the most wonderful job in the world, but somehow sellers just never get around to writing you a letter unless you ask for it. What's more, most people will write you a better letter if you ask for it than if they think of it themselves. Don't be afraid to ask. It really works.

You can also contact past buyers and sellers, which of course is a great way to prospect for new business. Ask them for a letter as well.

Keep adding letters to your book. This section can grow and grow, which greatly helps you sell yourself. When you've left your *Career Book* with homeowners, and they are reading all these wonderful letters that have been written about you, it has a fantastic impact! Every time a seller writes a letter about you it is as if they are writing an ad about you. The more letters you have, the better.

Now, if you are new in the business you might ask me, "Well, gee, Barb, I just started in real estate. I don't have any letters of recommendation yet." Then put in letters from your other careers. They will fit well in this section, too. They might help you strike a common bond with someone. Besides, they help you show that you are a reliable person. I assure you, a future seller will not read a letter written by IBM saying how great you are and think to themselves, "He was great at IBM, but he'll stink in real estate." People do not think that way. They assume you made the change for the better, not the worse, and they transfer the credibility you had in your last career to real estate.

Advertising and Open House Information. Remember, this is not a listing presentation book. However, I kept hearing the following from sellers, "Barb, we think you are great, but does your company really advertise? Will you hold an open house for us?" Remember the key to gaining control is to educate the sellers up front. Because most sellers think that the two things that sell homes are ads and open houses, I decided to head off their objections ahead of time. I did this by filling my book with lots of ads and open house invitations.

This is a prime opportunity for you to show off the advertising placed by you or your company. Put in copies of ads from different papers used by your company. Maybe these are ads you have placed yourself. Whether they are from a magazine or newspaper, black and white or color, make sure you include a strong sampling of recent ads. You can also put in open house invitations.

Photos of Listed and Sold Homes. This section is so powerful! Everyone knows a picture is worth a thousand words.

Let me tell you how this section came about in the first place. I had been using the other sections of my book as I have described them for quite a while, and my *Career Book* worked every time. One day when I came back to give a particular seller the Detailed Report, however, the sellers made a comment that changed my book (and now yours) forever. This particular seller said, "Barb, my wife and I think you're great. We trust you more than anybody else who has come through our home, because frankly, we now know more about you than any other agent. We've already decided to have you list our home because of that. But, there is something missing in your book that you really ought to add." I said, "Please tell me what that is. I really would like to know." He looked me square in the eyes and asked, "Lady, what have you ever sold, anyway?" At that moment I realized that sellers are also very interested in production.

So, I went out with my camera and took pictures of every home I had listed and put the photos in my book. No matter who sold the homes, they were my listings, so in my book they went. I also included any home that someone else had listed that I had sold. Now sellers could see my production.

Every home you list and sell goes in this section. You've told them about your background. You've shown them your résumé. You've shown them pictures of your family. They've seen your company ads. They've seen the awards and credentials that you have in the business in addition to the ones you earned before you got into real estate. But you also want them to say to themselves, "This person knows what she is talking about when she talks to us about real estate. I can see that she really knows what she is doing. Here are some of the listings she has actually sold."

Highlight the neighborhoods and the price ranges in which you specialize. When I put in the homes that I have listed and sold, I put in individual information sheets on each property. In my own book, I also put the price for which a house listed or sold. I suggest that you put in one or the other. Either white out the listing price and just put the selling price, or show what it listed for and do not tell them the selling price. For example, I put, "Listed for $95,000. Sold to an out-of-town purchaser, and was financed with VA financing." On another home, if I were to white out the listing price, I would just say, "Sold $185,000, to an out-of-town purchaser with conventional terms." I usually write that in longhand, or type it in on the information sheet I used when I marketed the property.

This is truly a powerful section! Sellers love seeing all the pictures of the homes you've sold. If you have been in business for fifteen years and sold the same home three times, then take three pictures of it and write under each picture about each sale. Dynamite! Be sure to represent all the markets you work. If you work in the high end only, don't put in the one low-end sale you had. If you work in the low end don't put in the one high-end sale you had. But, if you focus on people rather than on properties then represent all market ranges in your book. I have sales in my book from $35,000 all the way into the millions of dollars. I have many resale homes in my book, new construction, townhouses and condominiums, vacant lots and acreage, even horse ranches and farms. I want it all covered. Put in the commercial sales you've had, too. You never know when the person you leave it with may be an investor or know someone else who is.

As your book grows, you eventually won't even have room for all of your listings sold and sales to go in your book. You also don't want to overwhelm the reader. Therefore, I keep the most recent sales I have had and a representation at all times of the various markets and price ranges in which I work.

Take photos. Fill your *Career Book* with them, and they will take you to the bank!

Other Homes You Have Listed. Be sure to include information and pictures of the homes you currently have listed. People are reassured by the fact you have other clients, and they love to see other homes and properties you have listed. I have actually had sellers want to see a listing that was in my *Career Book*, and I have ended up selling it to them. This has happened several times each year. Incidentally, these are some of the easiest sales I have ever made.

Winning Idea for Those New to Real Estate. If you are brand new you may not have any listings or sales, or very few. How do you achieve credibility in these areas? When I first went into real estate, I didn't have any sales to go in my book either. I came up with the idea of a title page that talked about the company listings. I asked other agents in my office if I could take pictures of their listings. I put the pictures in this section of my book with my card on each page. I said to the agents, "Who knows, maybe I can sell one of your listings and then we will both make money." Meanwhile, this section helped me gain credibility at the same time. It worked. I did sell several of the other agents' listings. As I got my sales and they closed, I added the sold section to my book that I've already described. As I got my own listings, I added that section as well.

Ending the Book. One of the best ways I know to end your *Career Book* is to put in a photo of yourself with a "SOLD" sign. Here's how to do it. The next time you go out on a company tour have an associate take your picture standing in front of a house alongside your company sign with "SOLD" attached. It's easy! Don't show the whole house. In fact, it doesn't even have to be for sale. This photo is for public relations and the important thing you want to show is you and the sign. The house will become a blurred background and that's just fine.

Take several shots so you can choose the best one for your book. Once you pick the one you like, blow it up to 8 × 10 and put it in your *Career Book*. It will make a powerful statement about you to end the book. "I sell homes" is the message and a picture like this will get it across loud and clear.

SIMPLE BUT CRUCIAL PROCEDURE

Preparing a real estate *Career Book* about yourself is as simple as collecting the material and following the order I've outlined. You may want to rearrange it a little to suit your needs. There is no right or wrong way to do it. Anything that you feel comfortable sharing about yourself is great. Do what fits you, but do it! Don't wait until your book is perfect. You are perfect in your own way right now. I really believe that. Even a partially finished book will bring you great rewards. Just get your book together, and get it out there so it can go to work for you now. Sometimes I will meet someone who got a *Career Book* from me and they will say to me, "I'm not using my book yet because it isn't quite good enough" or "it isn't quite finished yet." Think of the business they are missing while they are trying to make it perfect or while they are procrastinating. Procrastination is the biggest killer of sales. Don't put off what you can do today. Get your book together, and get your sales going. It works everytime!

The *Career Book*, like you, should constantly be growing and changing. I am always adding new listings and "SOLD" homes to my *Career Book*. I continue to collect new information all the time and keep it in a drawer in my desk at work. Then one night each quarter, I take all my odds and ends home to bed and update my *Career Book* on my lap, while I watch Johnny Carson on TV. It's easy! So, get started now. You will be amazed at how much the *Career Book* will help you sell yourself and build your career.

Who should build a *Career Book*? Anyone can build a *Career Book*.

Let me share a true story with you that happened at one of my seminars. The day was over, and everybody was gone. It must have been about half past five in the evening. I was packing up to leave, and I didn't realize anyone else was still in the room. Then this slender, blonde-haired woman approached me. She said, "Can I talk to you a minute?" I said, "Sure. What would you like to talk about?" The large ballroom was completely empty, but she didn't want to talk with me out in the open. She literally took my hand and said, "Let's talk over here behind this partition, if you don't mind." I didn't know what she was going to do. As we walked behind the partition she said, "I loved your program today, but there is one thing I have a real problem with. There is one thing I just can't do." I asked, "Are you new in the business?" She said, "Yes I am new." I continued, "Are you a little worried about *Staging* homes? Is that it?" She said, "No, I think I can really *Stage* homes after spending today with you. That's not it. The problem is that I am the only one here today that cannot put together a *Career Book*." I said, "Oh, sure you can. Anybody can put a *Career Book* together. Everybody should! What you want to do is put in a lot of pictures. Pictures are great. Then, list the clients that you had in your last career. They are great names for references. Oh, and get letters of recommendation and fill your book."

She repeated, "No, I can't. You just don't understand. I just can't do it." Now by this time she was getting red in the face, and her voice was getting a little louder and a little shaky. "Well," I said, "I guess I don't understand. Help me." What came out of her mouth next no one has ever said to me before. Because this woman stood up straight, put her shoulders back, looked me square in the eyes and said, "Well, you see Barb, this is kind of hard for me to say, but for the last eight years, ah, ah, for the last eight years I've been a prostitute."

You could have knocked me over with a toothpick. But think of the courage it took for her to say this to me. I stood there thinking of what to say. Then all of a sudden I looked her right back in the eyes and said, "Wel-1-1-1 listen, you have better people skills than anyone else who was here today." It was all I could think to say. Then I added, "You told me you learned a lot today. So, go home and type up what you learned and put it in your book. You have certificates of clock hours, so put those in. You got a certificate from me today, too. Do you have children?" She said, "Yes." "Well, put your kids in your book. And your pets too. You can get company listings and company ads, and before you know it your book will be full. You can put a book together!" By the time this woman left she really felt she could put a *Career Book* together and was on her way home to start it then. The beautiful thing, I thought, was that this woman was changing her whole life, which really took a lot of courage and guts. I give her all the credit in the world. Even though I haven't seen her since that day, I did receive a letter about a year later thanking me and telling me she had just been awarded the top production award in her office. She had married and was taking her husband and children to Bermuda, which was the prize for the top producer that year. How wonderful!

What do you want to happen this year in your life? You can make whatever you want to happen. I really do believe this. I truly believe that God has given us the greatest computer in the world and they haven't replaced it yet, have they? You have the power inside of you to do it. It is already there. The key is that you have to want to make the change. You have to want to do it, whatever it is, to make it happen. Now I want to give you a challenge from the true story I have just shared with you.

If the woman in the preceding story can put together a *Career Book,* I KNOW you can do it too! But you've got to *want* to put it together.

GUARANTEED SUCCESS

I can't urge you enough to put a book together. If you have one already, I know that it is out there earning you more money than you have ever made before. If you have not yet started a *Career Book*, get to work and get it done! I promise you, when you use your book correctly, you will make more money than you have ever imagined possible.

Do it now!

Prospecting and Uses of the Career Book®

In this chapter you will learn

1. The six major uses of the *Career Book*.
2. How to prospect using the *Career Book*.
3. How to knock on one door and reach thousands of people at a time using your *Career Book*. It all starts with someone you already know!

Marketing is the name of the game. This principle is true in real estate or any sales field. The company you work for right now most likely knows how to market. They splash their name anywhere and everywhere they can get it. They spend thousands, even millions, in some cases, on name familiarity, public relations, and marketing. This is one of the reasons you are with them right now. But how about you? What kind of marketing do you do on a regular basis? Most of us would not or could not afford to take out a full-page ad in the Sunday newspaper about ourselves. You just wouldn't do it. I really think that we leave too much of our marketing up to the company. We cannot sit in our offices anymore and say to an associate, "Do you see they gave another referral to Mary Jane! What has she got going with the manager anyway?" It is time we start to market ourselves in addition to what our company is already doing.

One of the facts I discussed in the last chapter was that the sellers you meet pick you and not the company. You need to market *you*. I think that the *Career Book* is the best marketing idea and tool in the industry today. It sells and markets you wherever and whenever you leave it. The *Career Book* is your walking résumé, a silent talker that speaks for you. It is a hardback definition of who you are and how you work. You can take it with you everywhere. You can loan it to everyone you know. Once you start circulating your *Career Book*, believe me, prospects will find you! Because your *Career Book* tells people exactly who you are and ways you have sold homes for other people, and it shows all the reasons people should hire you to list their property or sell them a property.

How many places can you be in at once? Your answer is probably "One." There is only one of you. But by using your *Career Book*, you will see how many places you can be at the same time. The more books you put together and leave with clients, the more places you can be at the same time.

It does so much more than your business card could ever do. There is no way you can put all the information we talked about in the last chapter on your business card, or even in a personal brochure. The *Career Book* is now the marketing tool that will bring you countless clients and customers. The number one thing you are selling is yourself. And, if you don't do it who else will?

How can you use your *Career Book* to prospect, and who are your prospects?

Finding prospects is mostly a matter of recognizing who your prospects are. You may not know this, but you are surrounded by prospects. They might be people you have never considered as potential clients. Even those people who aren't prospects right now can probably lead you to someone who is. Many times it starts with someone you know, which makes prospecting less scary. I want to share my list of solid sources for prospects that can keep you busy until you are ready to retire. I have developed these over the years using my *Career Book* and believe me they are solid prospect sources that can take you to the bank over and over again. You can do all your prospecting without a *Career Book*, but it's definitely not going to be as powerful. This is where you find the business.

SOURCE 1: SELLERS

Sellers! Sellers! Sellers!

I would never go to see potential sellers without my *Career Book*. Period.

Other agents will go to see the seller, leave their business card, and when they go they are gone. You leave your *Career Book*, and you are "living" in their home! I have never had potential sellers list with someone else as my book lay in their home. One seller even said to me, "Barb, we got to know you so well, we took you to bed with us last night." How can you beat that? Of course you are going to list their home, now that they know all about you. Therefore they like and trust you much more than the rest. They always find some common ground with you from looking through your book. It really puts the humanness back into selling yourself.

Imagine that I left my *Career Book* and you didn't. Who do you think will get the listing? You decide.

SOURCE 2: BUYERS

Of course, show your *Career Book* to buyers. We need them to "buy" into us too, don't we? Buyers only know what they see when they look at us, just like sellers. We need credibility when we work with buyers as well. Think about it: You send a relocation packet to out-of-town buyers; then they come to town actually to buy a home, and they know more about the town and your company than they do about you. You know all about them ahead of time, but they know nothing about you. Then we wonder why we have trouble getting and keeping the loyalty from our buyers. Credibility. It is the key.

Ask out-of-town purchasers to look at your book overnight when you drop them off at their hotel. Ask them to look through it and then return it to you in the morning when you pick them up to look at homes. Simply explain to the purchasers, "You know Mr. and Mrs. Purchaser, I know a lot about you. I know your wants and needs and all about your family. But you really don't know much about me, do you? I want you to trust my ability to find, show, and sell you your new home. So, I have put together a book about who I am and what I have done in real estate including some of the homes I have sold, my background, and even my family. I'd really appreciate your taking it up to your hotel room this evening and looking through it. It will help you get to know me so much better. I also show it to sellers that I work with as well." I've never had a buyer say no to looking at my *Career Book*. Why should they? You show me a buyer who says no and I'll show you someone who is not a serious buyer!

Local purchasers need to know about you, too. Don't put them in your conference room and give them an advertising magazine right away. All they'll do is find twenty-five more houses they want to see. Instead of that, give them your *Career Book*. Ask them to look through it while you set a couple more appointments for homes you are going to show them. It works every time to help you sell yourself to the buyers.

Now you will have common ground and credibility with them and your closing ratio with buyers will go up. Remember, too, buyers will become sellers before you know it. If they know you and your professionalism, who else would they call when they decide to sell?

SOURCE 3: FOR SALE BY OWNERS

For Sale by Owners are wonderful! They need you. They are a great source for listings. I built my listing career on For Sale by Owners. I used to knock on their doors and think to myself,

"I have to list this house or I'll die." Have you ever thought that at one time or another? Why do we do that to ourselves? We haven't even met the sellers or seen the house yet. So, I decided to work on one goal at a time and it worked. As I knock on someone's door my only goal is to get inside the house. When I first talk to these owners I express my interest in their neighborhood. I tell them that I have sold homes in the area and would love to see their home to keep up with the neighborhood. Almost all sellers will let me inside their homes. They just say, "Fine, you can look at my home, but I'm not listing it." I acknowledge their right to sell their home themselves and that I know how much work it is. I *never* say the word "list" the first time I visit a For Sale by Owner. It's a dirty word to them at this point.

I have my *Career Book* in my arms, and I carry it with me as I look through the home with them. I am thinking to myself, "Is this a seller I would like to work with and a home that I would like to list?" Remember, we are the executives. The sellers not only pick us, we also pick them. If this is a home I would want to list, then, I want to leave my book with them. This is my next goal.

Now, when it comes to For Sale by Owners I do not use the name *Career Book*. I call it "a book that has tips on selling in it." When you say tips on selling to these owners you definitely will get their attention. They usually say, "You have a book with tips on selling in it!" I then tell them that I have left my book with many other For Sale by Owners, and it has actually helped some of them sell their homes. I say that I don't have to show them the book, but rather I'll just leave it so they can look through it on their own. This really takes any pressure off, and I have never had a For Sale by Owner turn me down. They like the idea of looking through it on their own. The book isn't the pressure to them that you and I are anyway, because books can't talk back. I always tell them that there are pictures and information about other homes that I have sold in my book, and that I think they will enjoy looking at it. Some of the For Sale by Owners have almost torn it out of my hands. Once I give it to them, I also inform the owners that the book contains information about me that will also help them to know me better.

Now, if you will try this approach with For Sale by Owners you will learn what I have learned. Your *Career Book* is now "living" in the house. Both sellers look at it. Their children look at it. I have even had them loan it to neighbors because they were so impressed. The beautiful part is that other agents may come and go. They leave their business cards with the sellers, and when they go they are gone. Meanwhile, you will have the definite overall advantage because you are "living" in the house. I have never had a For Sale by Owner list with someone else when my book was in their home.

The key here, once again, is building credibility. These owners always find some kind of common ground in your *Career Book*. It never fails. They also tend to look on you as someone they now know. How can someone else's business card compete with your book? Impossible. It can't even begin to touch it. Now when you return to pick up your book, the negatives they may have thought or expressed before are gone.

This brings me to another important point. You have a perfectly logical reason to return, and that is to pick up your book. It is so easy and simple, and it really works. This gets you back in the house for the second time without the sellers saying, as they open the front door, "What are you doing here? I told you we are not listing our house." Not only do they not say this, but they welcome you with open arms. Again, the common ground in your book bridges the credibility gap. Only then do I ask the For Sale by Owner for an appointment to return and present my marketing program to them. I don't believe they realize my credibility is above many of the other agents in the area (remember the bottom five we talked about earlier) until I have left my *Career Book*. Now I am on the offense, not the defense. They may have turned me down earlier, but now they don't. Why? Because I have shown them my credibility through my book, and built more trust and common ground. It makes all the difference in the world. I then return at an agreed time to present my Detailed Report. I always tell these owners that I do not pressure people into listing with me. I don't need to because most of the sellers in my area are already pressuring *me* to list their homes. I go back to the office, put together the report and return to present it.

This, then, almost always leads to listing the For Sale by Owner. I cannot stress too much that the reason I have been so successful in this area of listing is because of the credibility I have built with the *Career Book*. You can do it, too!

SOURCE 4: OPEN HOUSES

I had my *Career Books* in my car for almost a year before I ever thought of taking them into my open houses. How could I have been so slow to realize how great they would work there? Please, don't be slow as I was.

It dawned on me one day. I asked myself, what am I taking into the open house to market myself? I have my company sign out front showing the open house. I have the company brochure and my business cards. But they might even throw my cards out the window of the car as they drive down the freeway, or they might lose them between the seats in the car. Any way you look at it, I needed something more to market myself at the open houses, and they were sitting in my car! I started to bring at least two of my books to open houses. I gave them to people I really clicked with—you know, the people who give you their name, address, and phone number. You really are getting along well with them. They seem to like you, and you like them. But, now they are going to leave. Sending a *Career Book* with them made so much sense, and it worked. Because they had already given me their name, address, and phone number, they did not hesitate to take my *Career Book* with them. I would simply tell them that I would love the chance to work with them. I had something to show that would help them to know me better. Then I would give them my *Career Book.*

Remember, many of the people who are looking at open houses are also looking for a salesperson they like and trust to help them find a property or list theirs. Your *Career Book* will make that decision a snap.

I used to call all the people I met over the weekend in my open houses on the following Monday morning. You know what I was thinking when I called them: "Are they still interested? Are they still motivated?" Now, I didn't have to call them anymore. Because, I got to go over to their home on Tuesday or Wednesday evening for a perfectly logical reason. I had to go there to pick up my book. They expected me. Next thing you know, I was sitting in their living room, perhaps meeting the spouse I did not meet at the open house. I could then see their home in person and say, "Why don't you let me do a work-up on the amount of equity you really have to see if you can make the move?" That is exactly what I would end up doing. The next thing you know

I was listing their home and selling them another one. Try your *Career Book* at open houses. Once again, it works!

SOURCE 5: BUILDERS

Builders love the *Career Book*. Why? Because they are looking for a salesperson who knows about marketing. They realize that the *Career Book* is a marketing tool about you. They will respect you more than the other salespeople in your area if you put one together and show it to builders. I know because that is how I attracted the builders whose homes I listed.

Actually, the first builder I ever listed gave me the idea of showing him the book. A man in jeans and a T-shirt walked into my open house and said, "Are you Barb Schwarz?" I said, "I sure am." He then said, "Well, you don't know me, but I build a lot of houses in this area. One of my friends said I was supposed to look you up and ask for some darn book you've got. Where is it?" I was chuckling inside because I realized one of my other sellers must have told him about my *Career Book*. I gave it to him, and I went on to list for one of the best and most productive builders in my area. In fact, he called me in two days after taking my book with him. This was even before I could call him.

I got to thinking, as I worked with more and more builders, if the *Career Book* works for me why wouldn't it work for builders, too? So, I got my builders to give me their backgrounds in résumé form, all their own credentials, their family pictures, and letters from subcontractors they used in building their houses (and if the subs want to get paid they will write the letter, I promise you!). In addition, I took pictures of every house they had ever built in town (with the purchasing family in the front of the house) and included letters from families naming my builder as the best in the entire area. I put all of this in what I called the *Company Career Book*. Each builder had his own book, but I didn't let my builders keep the individual books I had put together for them. Rather, I kept them with me at all times. I would show them at any time to anyone, and I especially used them whenever I was holding a builder's open house on the weekends. As with my own book, my goal was to send the builder's book home with buyers who might be interested in having my builder build them a home— either a presale or a custom home. Do you know what started to happen? The buyers would literally start to fall in love with the builder's work, and I'd get a call that went something like this: "Barb, we met you in a builder's open house last week, and you gave us his *Company Career Book*. Well, we have looked through it several times and would like you to come over to our present home and talk to us about your builder doing a custom or presale home for us!"

In a nice way, it was like taking candy from a baby, because the book had done almost all of the selling for me. For any builder whose homes you currently list or that you will list in the future, I strongly urge you to do these two things: Show them your *Career Book*, and put together a *Company Career Book* for your builder. It makes so much sense, and it works.

SOURCE 6: ANYONE!

This source is my favorite. You can knock on one door and reach thousands at a time. It all starts with someone you know, so it is not scary.

In your area, to whom do you give business? I know you give out people's names because we are asked for them all the time in our business. "Do you know a good doctor? Do you know a reliable CPA in this area? Barb, I need a new dentist, one I could really trust that my kids would like." I got to thinking about all the business I hand out and how I never really ask for any of it back. Well, now is the time to change all of that. I made a list of people: my accountant, doctor, dentist, hairdresser, stock broker, insurance agent, banker, directors of major companies in town, and so forth. I then decided to do the following, which I strongly recommend to you because it works:

1. Call each of them up and ask him or her to lunch, one at a time.
2. As you take each one to lunch, take the time to make the point, over lunch, that you are so much different from most of the other agents they have ever worked with before. In other words, you will say, "Let me tell you how I work."
3. Ask for their account. If you don't ask, you may not get it. Remember, ask and you shall receive. But you have to ask!

Even though we are in sales, many of us simply forget to ask.

4. Give the person your *Career Book.* Ask him or her to take it back to work and pass it around. For example, I did this with my accountant and obtained his company's entire account of referral business. The key is that if you give them business, they will give you business back. It only makes good business sense. But again, you have to ask. The key is your *Career Book* because of the extra credibility it will build with these people.

Professional people want to refer their clients to a salesperson who is likable and trustworthy and will make them look good, not someone who will embarrass them. Do you know that some of these professionals actually asked me to put an extra book together for them to keep at their office to show their clients? Seeing my book ahead of time builds trust before they ever meet me. Terrific!

Spend the small amount of time it takes to put your own list together. Who can you take to lunch and ask to send you business? You know many more people than you even think you do. Networking and namedropping work. How about your accountant? I knew that mine did taxes for about fifteen other real estate agents. But I wondered if he really knew how differently I worked. So I took him to lunch one day to tell him. I left my *Career Book* with him. I talked to him later, and do you know what he said? He said, "I didn't know you did all of this production. Our clients are always looking for investments, buying and selling houses and property. I'm going to start sending them to you." You can do the same thing, so don't wait!

Try letting your attorney know what you do. Many times in divorce cases or other types of settlements, people need to sell their houses. If your attorney knows what you do, he will be more likely to spread your name around to clients. So take your attorney to lunch, tell him or her how you work, and leave your *Career Book* in his or her hands.

Leave your *Career Book* where you have your hair cut, where you bank, where you work out— everywhere! The more people who know how you work, the more leads you'll generate. People are usually happy to refer you, but they forget. It is our job to help them keep us in their minds at all times when thinking about real estate. They say that everyone on the face of the earth knows at least 250 other people. Think of the numbers you can reach by the method I just discussed. Your *Career Book* is a crucial tool as you do this, because it takes away any doubt that you are the right salesperson to receive their referrals and replaces it with credibility.

By the way, there is only one best place to keep your *Career Books* as you go about the business of real estate— in someone else's hands! In between, however, I have found the best place to keep them is in the back seat of my car. I got a box from the grocery store, put it in the back seat of my car, and put my *Career Books* there. Why? Because our cars are really our offices, aren't they? (By the way, if your trunk looks like mine, you don't want to keep them there. Also, out of sight means out of mind.) I wanted them with me at all times so I could hand them out at a moment's notice. If you leave them at your office, you'll forget them. I know because that's what I did. The same is true for leaving them at home. Keep them in your car.

One more tip would be to put each book in an old pillow case, in the box in the back seat. It helps prevent scratches and sticking together in hot weather.

Show your *Career Book* to your spouse and other family members. Ask your spouse to take it to work and pass it around at the office. If you take the time to prepare your book professionally, your spouse will be proud of your book. I decided to call my husband's secretary at work and ask her to be sure that my *Career Book* went all through the company, to every department and floor. She wants to do anything extra to please her boss. Right? It worked. I can't even begin to tell you all of the extra referrals I began to receive. Those referrals turned into many sales.

Let your neighbors know what you do. Think about it. Do your neighbors really know what you do? Tell them what you do... better yet, show them what you do in real estate by leaving your *Career Book* with them, one neighbor at a time. Chances are they will want to sell someday. Wouldn't you rather have them come to someone they know— you— instead of turning to strangers?

Remember, everyone knows at least 250 other people and that includes your neighbors. They know many other people in other neighborhoods that you don't know. Why not put these people into your hands as referrals from the neighbors you do know as a result of showing them your *Career Book?*

I can't say this enough: Prospects are everywhere because everyone is a prospect— if you let them know how you work. If you educate people and let them know what you can do for them, you can have as many prospects as you can handle. The *Career Book* is one of the best ways I know to let other people know what you do, and it's one of the most exciting parts of my listing program. Real estate salespeople everywhere tell me it is changing and helping them individually; they also say that this book is changing and helping our industry. At long last sellers have a proven way to find the agent who meets their needs. The day is really coming when the agent who does not have a *Career Book* will not get the listing because the business card is simply no match.

The *Career Book* is your walking résumé. It is a hardback definition of who you are and how you work. You take it with you everywhere. You loan it to everyone you know. Once you start circulating your *Career Book*, believe me, prospects will find you! Because your *Career Book* tells people exactly who you are and ways you have sold homes for and to other people. In other words, your *Career Book* shows all the reasons, in a simple but professional way, why someone should hire you to list his or her property.

Get your *Career Book* together and out there prospecting for you. It is now possible to be in more than one place at the same time, and it works. Prospecting with your *Career Book* is fun, easy, and profitable. It will truly "TAKE YOU TO THE BANK."

6

Step 2:
The Detailed Report

In this chapter you will learn

1. How to set the *Stage* for your presentation
2. Two parts of the Detailed Report (listing presentation)

Educating your sellers is the key to getting "Yes!" listings—homes that look great and are priced to sell. Your greatest opportunity for educating your sellers is during your listing presentation, which I call the Detailed Report.

The best presentation is one that explains the listing process to sellers as well as informs them of your skills as a listing agent. To be able to accomplish both these objectives you must be willing to spend time preparing and practicing your listing presentation, in addition to spending at least an hour and a half giving a presentation to your sellers.

The Detailed Report (or listing presentation) contains two important parts: Part One is your Exclusive Marketing Program and Part Two is your Comparative Market Analysis (CMA). Each part is crucial to educating the seller as to how you work and all the service you provide.

Many times we say more than we think we do. We make statements with our bodies. So, it is a good idea to be aware of what signals you are sending with your body language, and what others' movements are telling you.

Knowing where to sit and where to have your sellers sit is very important for maintaining professional control during your listing presentation.

What do you include in your report (or presentation)? There are definite facts and pieces of information that you need to share with your sellers. This is where education of the sellers is crucial. Here is where we can end objections before they ever think of them. What you teach your sellers during your presentation can literally determine whether or not you become the listing agent for those sellers.

SETTING THE STAGE FOR PRESENTATION

Notice I used the word *Stage*. You can *Stage* anything. *Stage* your car. *Stage* your appearance. *Stage* the sellers' home and *Stage* your presentation. It is very important.

The Right Touch

I want to show you some ways you can add more power to your listing presentation. I'm talking about the small details. Do you ever think about how you actually conduct your presentation? Do you pay attention to body language, where you sit, where the sellers sit, and so forth? You might think these are all items of very little importance, but they can make a big difference.

Greeting

Let's say it's time to go to the sellers' home for your listing presentation, which I call the Detailed Report. You have your complete presentation, which is your Exclusive Marketing Program, Comparative Market Analysis, and *Marketing Portfolio* as you approach the door and ring the doorbell. (In the next chapter we will cover the *Marketing Portfolio* in detail.) When the sellers come to the door, extend your hand, and say something like, "Oh, it's great to see you again." Of course, they invite you inside the house. Now, remember, you sat in the living room for the first visit, but I recommend that you not sit in the living room again until the sale is closed and they have the proceeds from the sale of their home in their hands.

Location of Meeting

Always say to your potential sellers, "Could we sit at the kitchen table?" Then go into the kitchen to sit down. Sometimes they might say, "Let's sit at the dining room table." Explain to the sellers that's fine, but that you don't want to scratch it. Tell them that unless they have a table cloth or table pad, you would rather give your presentation in the kitchen. The important thing is that you are all comfortable and you don't have to stretch out your presentation materials from a sofa to an easy chair in the living room. No one can give a professional presentation and maintain the necessary control sprawling from a wing back chair to the living room sofa across a coffee table. You just can't do it. From now on, use the kitchen table or a covered dining room table as your workstation with your sellers. All the work you do in the future should be conducted at the same table. You are setting the *Stage* for work. It doesn't really matter where the table is as long as there are as few distractions as possible. Round tables are better than those with corners.

Placement and Body Language

Body language is crucial. I believe in placing people where I can be most effective with them and for them. For example, let's say you go to make a presentation and think that the wife is more dominant and outgoing than the husband. Sit closer to her. If you think the husband is the decision maker, sit by him. By sitting closer to the person who seems to have the most authority, you can use that power to control the flow and mood of your presentation. To do this, when the woman is the dominant one, ask her where she usually sits at the table. Like most of us, she probably has her own seat. Then, have her husband sit on one side of her, and you sit on the other side. That way, she is in the middle. Now, why does it matter if you sit beside the wife? Well, if she is the decision maker and she starts to get out of control, because of pricing or anything you talk about, she is much easier to control because you are beside her. You can even pat her elbow a little and talk her through the problem. If she is across from you, there is no way you can calm her down as easily or keep the situation under control. If the husband is the decision maker, you simply reverse the placement I have just described.

A quick tip: I believe in touching, and I believe it can really help you in real estate sales, if you do it the right way. I believe you can touch people in a professional, nonthreatening way to help you get your message across. A touch on the elbow or a light hand on the shoulder can have a calming effect and can help build rapport. I have also found that in the beginning, as I work with sellers and touch them on the shoulder or elbow, I do not look them in the eyes. I simply look toward the object I am talking about (such as a mantle on the fireplace or comparable homes in the market analysis) and reach out for their elbow or shoulder at the same time. Contact with the eyes is more intimate than touch, and I don't combine the two when I work with sellers in the beginning.

Of course, you want to be careful not to invade a seller's personal space. We all have a certain amount of space around us, and if someone breaks the barrier of that space, we put up our defenses. For example, think of how you would feel if you were in line at the grocery store and the person behind you kept looking over your shoulder as you wrote a check to pay your bill. You don't want to put your sellers on the defensive. So, be very subtle when touching them. If you feel comfortable doing this just offer a reassuring pat now and then. If you don't feel comfortable doing this, then don't do it. For touching to work, you have to feel natural doing this; otherwise, forget it. I would never want you to do anything that you did not feel comfortable with because it will come across loud and clear to sellers.

When setting the *Stage*, you have to be careful not to invoke jealousy. For example, I am a female, and the wife is a female. It would not matter if I were twenty, forty, or seventy-nine years old. It does not matter how I look. I must be very careful to not pay too much attention to the husband. If he is sitting beside me and I don't pay any attention to her, guess what is going to happen? She may become jealous. When I leave, she may say to him, "There is no way that woman is listing our house!" I do not want female sellers saying that because they felt I was too attentive to their husbands. Male agents have to be aware of the same thing if they are working with a woman. Be attuned to how your actions are being perceived. Pay equal attention to both partners.

Place people where you want them, but do be aware of your body language and what it is saying about you. Listen to what their actions tell you, and be careful that your actions don't say the wrong things. You don't want to inadvertently insult a potential seller. No matter what company you work for, you are still representing yourself and your company. Talk as a professional and behave as a professional.

CONTROL OF FLOW

Although your sellers are ultimately your employers, you have to control the presentation if you are to do your best job. In the end this is the best for them. It is your show. You worked hard, you did extra research to be sure your price recommendation was accurate, and you stayed late at the office to prepare your report for the sellers. Perhaps you didn't get to go to the movies with your family. So why give a presentation unless you set the *Stage*, give the introduction, and be the keynote speaker? It only makes good business sense.

Also, as you give your report you need to be the one turning the pages. I once had a seller (the only one like this I've had in all my years of selling) who just didn't want to wait. I was in the middle of my presentation, and I could just tell he was really excited. He loved everything, but he just couldn't wait. So, he leaned over and started to turn my pages to peek at what was coming next. I thought, "He's going to see the price, and he is going to be shocked." So, I just put my hand down on the page very calmly, and I said, "Joe, you know, there are special things I want to share with you on every page, and don't you worry, we're going to get there. So, hang in there with me, OK?" He said, "OK, Barb" and put his hands back in his lap, and I went on with the presentation. So, if things start to get out of control a little, you have to get that control right back. The flow and timing of your presentation are very important.

If the kids come in and interrupt the flow of your presentation, stop. Let them talk to the parents. Let the parents handle that situation. Whatever the interruption, let the sellers take care of it before you go on. If one seller leaves the table to take care of a child or a phone call *don't go on.* Wait until he or she returns to go on with your presentation. Talk to the remaining seller about the weather, sports, anything, but not the presentation. It doesn't do you any good to make a presentation if you don't have all your sellers' undivided attention. Remember, they don't know what you don't tell them!

LANGUAGE

The words you use when talking to sellers can have a profound effect on whether they accept or reject what you are telling them. I believe you can tell sellers anything. It isn't what you say, it's how you say it. No matter what you are sharing with the sellers always represent yourself in the most professional way possible. Otherwise, things we say that are not professional may come back to haunt us later. We must always be personable but professional. For example, I love the word "transaction." In my mind, that is the most effective word we can use. The word— I almost hate to say it— "deal" does not belong in the world of real estate.

Use "professional fee" or "brokerage" instead of "commission." Commission sounds hard against a seller's ears.

When you put a document in front of someone, always say, "Will you please authorize this for me?" Or "Will you please approve this agreement?" That sounds so much softer than, "Sign here."

The word "agreement" is so much more pleasant than "contract." That's what you do— come to an agreement.

By all means, share stories with sellers. I call them war stories. We've all gone through challenging and interesting situations. Funny things happen. Sad things happen. Stories about these situations lend credibility to your character, add strength to your presentation, and help you illustrate your point.

PRACTICE MAKES PERFECT—AND INCREASES INCOME!

What is your average individual brokerage commission per listing or sale? Have you ever taken the time to figure that out for yourself? In most areas of the United States, the average sales commission you earn can be approximately $2,500 per listing sold. Some areas are higher; others are lower. Let's just use $2,500 for an example. Every time you give a Detailed Report you could be earning that $2,500 if you are successful. If you were asked to give an hour-and-a-half talk for $2,500, it would be safe to assume you would practice that speech, right? Not only would you practice it once, you would probably practice it over and over again. Why do we tend never to practice in real estate? Actually, we do practice but we practice on the very person who is going to be our employer— our future sellers. Practice does make perfect. So, practice your presentation and then practice it again and again. Make sure it is perfect *before* you try it on sellers. It will get you more listings and sellers that are properly educated.

Think of your presentation as a $1,500 to $4,000 speech. If the seller is motivated by your speech, you will get the listing. With that kind of income at stake, doesn't it make sense to practice your presentation?

If you want to get more listings and sales, heed this advice: Take what you learn from this book, develop your own presentation in your own style, and practice. Practice until your presentation is natural and smooth. Practice alone. Practice with people in your family. Know your material so well you can be flexible enough to handle interruptions and answer questions, and relaxed enough to put the sellers at ease. The individual with the strongest and most educational presentation for the sellers will usually get the listing.

PARTS OF THE PRESENTATION

Remember, with every listing presentation you give, you are marketing yourself and your service. By using a professionally prepared marketing program, a *Marketing Portfolio*, and a well-rehearsed verbal presentation, you decrease the chance of misunderstandings and capitalize on your professionalism as a licensed real estate agent. If you will use these presentation ideas, you will be listing more houses than ever— and making more money! Remember, it is your show and your income. I want you to make money and stay in this wonderful business!

Two Parts of the Detailed Report

At the end of this section, you will see a list of the different parts of the Detailed Report. These are my suggestions to you. I know that you probably already have a presentation or are forming one for yourself at this time. Look at what I have in my report to the sellers and compare it with yours; see what you might add to make your presentation even stronger. I have also found that the order of items you see on my suggested list really works. By giving a Detailed Report in this order, your presentation logically unfolds in front of the sellers. They love it and, more important, they are totally educated on both marketing and pricing. The two parts of the listing presentation follow.

Part One

- Cover page for your Exclusive Marketing Program.
- Letter of introduction and your company's information.
- Exclusive Marketing Program for sale of home (use with the *Marketing Portfolio*).
- *Marketing Portfolio* (use with the Exclusive Marketing Program).

- Tips for selling.
- Property records from the county.
- Loan information letter.

Part Two

- Comparative Market Analysis cover page.
- Estimate of sellers net proceeds form. (I like to leave this form blank and fill it in with the sellers as we zero in on their list price at the end of my presentation.)
- Multiple listing service weekly statistics.
- Solds, expireds, and off-the-market comparables.
- On-market comparables.
- Recipe for a sale.
- Pricing your home using the market position triangle.
- Listing agreement.

As we progress together in the chapters to come we will take a detailed look at all of these materials. As I come to see the sellers for Step 2, the Detailed Report, all of the preceding information is in the listing packet I bring with me. I also bring my *Marketing Portfolio* to show the sellers samples of the work I am going to promise them that I will do. You will soon learn why and how this is so powerful. Notice in the two parts of the report that the price is next to the very last piece of paper I show the sellers (the very last piece of paper is the actual listing agreement, which I have already shown them a copy of earlier in the presentation to remove some of the fear of the "paperwork"). I leave the price to the last because I want to thoroughly educate them as to how and why I arrived at the suggested list price before I ever show it to them. In more than ten years in this business, I have never had a seller want to skip the presentation and say, "Just give me the price." I think this is because I have taught them up front in "Let me tell you how I work" that they deserve to know everything. They owe it to themselves. This works, and they not only remember it but expect it from me. This gives us the edge to get the listing because many other agents won't take the time to educate the sellers up front and show this type of Detailed Report.

Take time to educate your sellers. No one on the face of the earth can educate a seller as to the marketing he or she will do in fifteen minutes, because agents who are only doing fifteen minutes of marketing in this day and age will not get the listing any more. Sellers deserve it. We owe it to them. You will benefit by getting the listing, having the control you need to price it right and get the house *Staged* for sale, and then "taking it to the bank."

7

The Marketing Portfolio™

In this chapter you will learn

1. How and why the *Marketing Portfolio* was developed.
2. How to develop and use your own *Marketing Portfolio.*
3. Why your marketing presentation should be a "show-and-tell" presentation.

To sell yourself as a listing agent, you have to be able to show your sellers what you have done for other homeowners who have sold their homes and what you will do for them. The *Marketing Portfolio* is the best way to do this.

MARKETING PORTFOLIO

If you were excited about the *Career Book*, hold onto your hat. What I am going to tell you now is just as powerful as the *Career Book*, yet for an entirely different purpose. I'm talking about the *Marketing Portfolio*, which is a special, personalized listing presentation book. By the time you finish reading this chapter, every time you see or hear the words *Marketing Portfolio* you're going to think dollar signs because of the listings it will bring you!

Seed of a Sample Book

In the beginning, it was very simple. I wrote out my marketing program— all of the things I would do to market a property. I would type up the list and sign my name to it. This then was my commitment to the sellers in writing. Then I started to bring samples of my work with me to my listing presentations. I did this because I could see that sellers did not always really understand my marketing techniques if I just told them. They wanted to see samples of my work. How did I know that? Because they asked me to bring samples of my work with me. I just called it "my sample book." It was actually in a small folder containing a few papers: a copy of a flyer, maybe a bulletin or two, a copy of an ad, and even a letter I had written to another agent about someone's property. I had just a few simple things to show potential sellers what I would do to market their properties. But do you know what? Showing the sellers samples of my work really worked— even at that point. It began to help sellers see what I was talking about and helped them understand the importance of my many marketing techniques. So, I made it a permanent part of my presentation. It added weight to my marketing program, and I listed more and more homes. That little folder grew into the *Marketing Portfolio* and I know that the concept can help you give a more powerful presentation and get more listings.

During the years as I refined the *Marketing Portfolio* I started to include more samples of the marketing techniques that I used. It naturally evolved into sections so I designed divider pages to cover each technique. The more I educated my future sellers with examples of the work I would do for them, the more professional control I had. I wouldn't give a listing presentation without it now, because the *Marketing Portfolio* is so powerful. I know that once you fully understand its merits you won't give a listing presentation without it either.

As I go from city to city, I see different companies and agents all over our great country and all the different materials they use. The *Marketing Portfolio* is personalized to show off the marketing techniques *you* use. That's the beauty of it! It is the work you do— not just what the company does— as a real estate agent working for an individual seller. If you have a company book, you can add these ideas to it. But, in my mind, the best way to make an excellent impression is to use the book as a separate presentation book. It shows off what you as an individual agent, together with your own company, have done in the past, as well as what you will do for the sellers in the future as you decide to work together as a seller-and-agent team.

Do not ever leave your *Marketing Portfolio* with the sellers as you do with your *Career Book*. Rather, bring it with you for Step 2, and use it as a part of your listing presentation. In the next chapter I will show you exactly where the *Marketing Portfolio* fits into your listing presentation and ways to use it to showcase your work. It is an excellent tool for educating your sellers— and selling your service!

Show and tell = success.

The *Marketing Portfolio* is in the same order as the marketing program I am going to outline for you in the next chapter. This is important to remember. The marketing program tells them what you are going to do, and the *Marketing Portfolio* shows them what you are going to do. It covers your work from the very beginning when you first meet the sellers all the way through to a closed sale.

Now, let's go through the concept of the *Marketing Portfolio*, and I'll give you ideas on what you can show your sellers to make your listing presentation the most powerful it can be. You can make your own sample book and use all the ideas in this chapter, or you can use my *Marketing Portfolio*.

START WITH YOUR COMPANY

Your company is important. It's important to you or you wouldn't be with them. It's important to your sellers too, because they want to be reassured that they are with the best company and salesperson to sell their home. The rest of the *Marketing Portfolio* is primarily about you and your individual techniques, but I think it's good to start your book by including information about your company. Include things such as company pamphlets, newspaper articles, awards, pictures, and so forth. Show off the company. Let your sellers know why you work there, and why it's such a great company for you and for them.

LISTING PROCESS

Next, start showing your sellers the process you go through to actually bring their property on the market. In the beginning of your *Marketing Portfolio* show a copy of the listing agreement the multiple listing service uses in your area. If your company uses its own forms, display them in this section. I find that having a copy of the agreement here takes some of the fear out of the paperwork later. Take as much time as needed to discuss the form or simply let your future sellers know that this is the paperwork you will complete together in the future.

EDUCATE FUTURE SELLERS ABOUT STAGING HOMES

If you *Stage* homes (and I know you will after you finish this book), then this is the section in your *Marketing Portfolio* to show off that special service. Any tips for selling would go right behind this title page because preparing the home for sale is one of the first things to do for your sellers *after* completing the paperwork.

You can include company tip sheets or an article from the newspaper. The *Marketing Portfolio* comes with "Tips for Selling" that I have written.

One great idea is to include pictures of homes "before" and "after" they were prepared for sale. A picture is really worth a thousand words here, and it can actually be worth thousands of dollars for you. One sure way to get sellers to *Stage* their home is to show them pictures of other homes that have been *Staged.* Remember, sellers just need to be shown how and why *Staging* is so powerful and necessary. Money motivates most people and this means sellers as well. Teach them that a home that is prepared for sale, or *Staged,* will often sell quicker and in certain markets even for more money. Either way, they will be able to get their equity so much quicker if they prepare their home for sale. Many times, though, you have to be the one to teach them this because they won't think of it themselves.

Now you may be asking, "Barb, where am I going to get the before and after photos of homes?" This is easy. First of all, as you stage your next new listing or the one you now have that needs it, just ask the sellers if you can take photos before you *Stage* it together. I have never had a seller say no. Then, after it is *Staged* ask if you can take a second set of photos. Again, I have never had a seller say no. Then, I ask if I may show the photos to future sellers in our area after they have moved away. There is no reason for them to object because they will not live in the house anymore; some may not even live in the city anymore. Take photos before and after of the following rooms: living room, kitchen, master bedroom and bath, and the front of the home from across the street. These photos are the most powerful way to teach sellers about preparing their home for sale.

If you are new in real estate and don't have a listing that you can photograph, then take photos of your own house or apartment. That's right. Now don't misunderstand, I'm not suggesting that your home is messy. Just mess it up to make it look very lived in and then take your "before" photos. Then get it *Staged* to look more like a model home and take your "after" shots. The difference will be amazing, and your photos will really help to get your points across (they'll never know the photos were of your home). When you show your photos to sellers, tell them that the first one is an example of a room before it was *Staged* and the second is what it looked like afterward.

If you have sellers right now that will not prepare their home for sale, I would bet you haven't shown them before and after photos. Try it. It really does work. Put these photos in your *Marketing Portfolio* so that you don't forget to educate each and every one of your future sellers.

PROFESSIONAL INFORMATION SHEETS FOR SELLERS

Sellers deserve to be represented in the most professional way possible. This includes the information sheets that are left inside or outside your listings for buyers. Do your future sellers really know the quality of work you do in this area? Place samples of the professional information sheets you have written for past sellers' homes in your *Marketing Portfolio*.

I have come up with my own format for an information sheet that I know can help many agents. I do not simply use the standard information sheet from a multiple listing book. At the top of the information sheets I have pertinent information and facts that a purchaser can look at right away when he or she comes to view the property. Below that, I have a list of the unique features and special aspects of that property. Remember, good information sheets also help "sell" other agents as well as buyers. I promise the sellers, at this time, that this will be the type and quality of the work that I am committing to them. I show them that they will be represented in the most professional way possible. Educate. Educate. Educate.

SEPARATE MARKETING BOOKLET ABOUT EVERY LISTING

After the listing agreement is signed I make a separate marketing booklet for every one of my sellers. It is designed to be left in their home at all times. I therefore show a sample of one in this section of the *Marketing Portfolio* so they will fully understand its power. On the cover page it says "Do Not Remove." The booklet has all kinds of facts and features about the particular sellers' property. It includes the taxes, plat map, lender information, any disclosures, and a master copy of the information sheet I have prepared. Use your creativity, because anything that can help the buyer can be included. Consider including school information, churches, recreation, shopping, heating or air conditioning costs, copies of blueprints, landscaping plans, and so forth. The whole idea of the marketing booklet is to provide as much information about the property as possible. In the small space you are usually given through your multiple listing association, you may not be able to give agents all the information they want. I rely a great deal on other agents showing and selling my listings. I don't want them embarrassed by not knowing many of the answers to questions that purchasers might ask about the property. When they come to show one of Barb's houses, I want it to look terrific, but I also want the agent to be able to find the answers to questions a purchaser might ask.

This also gives you a marketing edge because you are promising the sellers something that many other agents haven't thought about doing. Sellers love it.

TEACH HOW THE MULTIPLE WORKS

I try to educate sellers about how the multiple listing service works. Without the sellers there would be no multiple. Let's not keep everything we do such a secret. In this section of the *Marketing Portfolio* I include a cover from one of our listing association books, maps that show the sellers the areas where most potential purchasers are looking today, and a sample of one of my listings as it is shown in the book. These samples show sellers how they will be represented. I purposely pick a listing that stands out and place it right in the middle of the page.

If you have the opportunity to buy supplements (extra spaces) in your MLS (some multiples call these addendums), do it. It is well worth the small cost because this is where we are marketing to each other. That is why we have a multiple. I personally buy that extra space for each one of my sellers. I also created a special border around my supplements. As my sellers, they deserve special treatment. Point out all the special things you do for them. They won't know how much extra work you do unless you tell them and show them.

WAYS BROKERS' OPEN HOUSES WORK

I believe in brokers' open houses. I can reach so many other purchasers by holding many brokers' open houses. Through brokers' open houses I reach the other agents in the multiple, and, therefore, reach their purchasers.

In my *Marketing Portfolio* I show a sample of the bulletin we get each week from our MLS and I show them the list of brokers' open houses and the results. Include examples of tour sheets or whatever method you use in your area to coordinate and advertise brokers' open houses. You can also use photos or flyers to show samples of activities promoting your own brokers' open houses.

If other agents in your area do not hold brokers' open houses, then this is something you can promise to your sellers that goes a step beyond. I did this in my own area, and then slowly other agents started holding more and more brokers' open houses.

Eventually, it became almost a standard. Agents that would not commit to holding brokers' open houses wouldn't get the listing. Brokers' open houses work.

QUALITY FLYERS

Flyers are wonderful! Show off examples of your best flyers in this section of your *Marketing Portfolio* to educate your sellers on the quality of the work you do. Also explain how flyers work, how many agents or offices you market to, and so forth. Take time to prepare your flyers for other agents because you are representing your sellers and yourself. Make it quality work— the best that you can do each and every time. Then you can offer sellers your highest level of marketing service, the one they deserve.

TOP-SELLING AGENT LIST

My mailing list has been an extremely effective marketing tool for me, and I hope you will use this idea to be even more successful. First, I want to tell you a little bit about how it

started. One day I thought to myself, "Where are today's purchasers?" I had a number of purchasers and a number of sellers,
but they didn't match. "Well," I answered my own question, "I
know where most of the purchasers are— they're working with
agents. But which agents?" I didn't know. I decided to check. I
got on the telephone and called every major broker or manager
in town. "Who are your top three selling agents?" I asked them.
"Which agents working with you primarily like to work with
buyers?" They could hardly wait to tell me. So, I compiled what
I called a list of the top fifty agents for that time in my area. I
started calling the agents. I asked them if I could put them on
a list and let them know about my listings because they were
priced right and prepared to come on the market (Staged). They
were flattered that I had called and glad to be on the list.

I started running off copies of the listings I had and mailed
those copies to the top 50 agents on a biweekly basis. That list
now has the names of 450 agents on it. I'm really proud of this
list. These people work hard to sell the listings I have. Why? For
several reasons.

1. They know my listings look good.
2. They know my listings are priced with the market.
3. They know my sales close.

I point out all those reasons to my sellers while I explain
my exclusive agent mailing list to them. A mailing goes out to
the top 450 agents in my multiple every three to four weeks.
They watch for the mailings. They show my listings from the
mailings, and they sell my listings from the mailings. Each seller
I show this technique to thinks it is dynamite! They know that
listing with me means they will be in the next mailing to those
top agents. In my mailings I use a copy of a flyer or an
information sheet on the home plus any extra information and
a photo. I use colored paper many times to attract attention on
agents' desks so my mailings will get opened instead of being
thrown away with all the rest of the individual flyers that tend
to stack up on their desks.

I also started the policy of sending agents a gift when they
sell one of my listings. On the day of closing the female agent
who sells one of my listings might get roses or a fruit basket,

whereas the male agent might receive a bottle or two of his favorite beverages, flowers, or a fruit basket. This policy has built a camaraderie for me and helped sell more homes for my sellers! It is such a small thing to do and yet many of us never really stop to thank the selling agent for bringing that buyer to our listing. Where would we be without each other? We really need each other. So the first person I am going to give a small gift to is not the buyer or the seller but rather the selling agent. You should see the stack of thank you notes I have gotten over the years from other agents who worked for other companies in my area! You better believe I show some of those to my sellers as well.

At the beginning of each new year I send a letter to each of the agents on my exclusive agent mailing list. Below is an example of the letter I send. I find it is a great way to get the year off to a positive start and remind them of our relationship in the past and how I hope we will have the chance to work together this year.

Dear Fellow Agents,

Happy New Year!
This past year was an exciting one in real estate in our area and I hope it was a very successful one for you. During the year I have been sending you information on the properties I have listed. I'm proud of the quality of listings that I always strive to obtain, and I want you to know that my listings will be easy for you to sell, because I work hard to price them right, *Stage* each listing, and help you close each and every transaction.
Thank you for showing and selling my listings. I'm going to continue to keep you informed this year so that you can show and sell my listings with confidence. I've enjoyed working with you, so please look for my listings so that we will have the opportunity of working together soon.
I wish you a happy and prosperous new year!

Sincerely,
Barb Schwarz

Have a copy of a letter like this one in your *Marketing Portfolio*, and show it to your sellers. Not only will they be impressed with your professionalism, but you are educating them on the importance of their property looking good and being priced right!

I have built a tremendous network of agents in the area where I work. In a way it is like having my own real estate company. It works because I have dozens of other agents constantly showing my listings. So start to build a network of agents in the area where you work. They can be with all types and sizes of companies. I'm not just talking about the company where you work; I'm talking about all the other companies around you. Strike up friendships. Meet other agents in the area where you live. Tell them, "I'll show your homes, if you'll show mine. Together we can make more money, and we can help out a lot more sellers that way." This really works.

In most multiples there are thousands of agents, and, of course, we can't get to know them all; however, you can build a strong network, and once you start it will grow. Once you get your sellers to prepare their homes for sale and agree to a reasonable price and terms, agents will love to show your properties. They can count on you to help them with the work.

So, in this section, put some of the letters you have written to other agents with other companies. Include a list of the names of agents you do business with in other companies. Display copies of the mailing labels or business cards to impress your potential sellers with the quantity of names you have on your marketing list. Then show examples of some of the mailings you have done to market your listings to these agents.

COMPANY ADVERTISEMENTS

Insert your company's ads from as many different kinds of media as possible. If you do individual ads on your own be sure to include samples of those as well. Put in the best advertisements you can find: black-and-white ads from the newspaper and color ads from magazines. Take the space to show off the quality of your advertising program, and explain how it works. If you send a newsletter to your centers of influence, be sure to add that as well.

Also, if you have had articles in the newspaper about any of the homes you have listed be sure that you include them in this section. Public relations and advertising let sellers know about what you and your company do.

RELOCATION

In the relocation section of your *Marketing Portfolio*, put information regarding the various relocation companies with which your own company may be associated. It is so crucial that sellers realize how relocation works and how buyers reach you through different relocation companies. Also, be sure you ask where your sellers are moving. You should always know where they are going. If they are moving out of the area or out of state it is a great way for you to also make additional income from referring them to an agent or firm out of your area. Too many agents simply let dollars slip through their hands by not even asking the sellers about their out-of-town move.

Another important reason to help sellers in this fashion is that you can put them in touch with a top agent in another area who can serve them. Don't leave sellers to their own luck in trying to find a top agent. As you know that is not always the easiest to do in a new area. By the way, this is one main reason that I have developed the Barb Schwarz Agent Referral Network.

As a speaker, trainer, teacher, and broker in the field of real estate I have had more than 100,000 of the best agents in the entire country take one of my full-day listing programs. I have reached more than 500,000 agents with my materials, audiotapes, and videotapes throughout their various companies. Great agents are always interested in referring sellers and buyers to other great agents in other states that are not in their own home markets. Therefore for years agents in other areas have called me at my office in Bellevue, Washington, and asked me for the names of agents that they could refer their clients and customers to in other areas and states.

They wanted the names of the agents who had taken my program. It was only a matter of time then until my own relocation network was born. Figure 7-1 shows the information that agents who participate in my relocation network include in their *Marketing Portfolio* to educate their sellers about the Barb

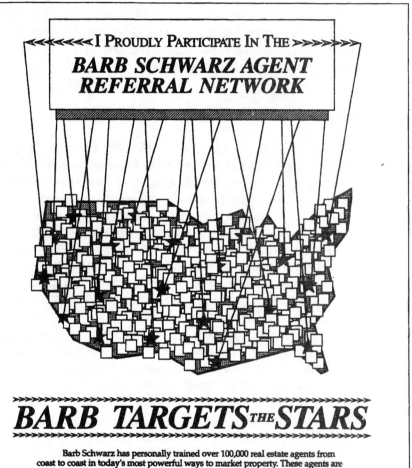

FIGURE 7-1 Barb Schwarz Agent Referral Network

Schwarz Agent Referral Network during their listing presentation, the Detailed Report. If you are interested in participating in my network please call my office telephone number, which is noted at the bottom of Figure 7-1.

It is the best way to rest assured that your referral will be taken care of by another great agent like you who knows how to *Stage* homes, and uses a *Career Book* and a *Marketing Portfolio* as you do.

BEST IDEA FOR SUSTAINING COMMUNICATION WITH SELLERS

Several years ago I thought to myself, "I do a lot of work for my sellers, and I am really proud of what I do. Sometimes however, they forget what I do, especially if their property hasn't sold yet, such as in a tough market. So, how can I let all of them know in a concrete way, consistently, what is being done to market their property?" I concluded that regular reports were the answer. So I decided to keep a log. All the marketing that I do for each property goes in the log. And I mean everything. I recommend you do the same thing. Just keep a spiral notebook in your car. Label every other page for each of the sellers you list and then write down everything you do. For example, let's say it's January 23.

- January 23— Met with Jane at her house to look at the property. I was there from 11 to 12:15.

Now, you see, I've just posted in two short sentences the work I just did. Let's say the next date is January 28.

- January 28— Met with Jane in my office from 9:30 to 11:00 to present my marketing program and my comparative market analysis. Agreed to meet on February 3 to list her home.

All I'm doing is listing everything I do. If it is a newspaper ad, I record it. If I held a brokers' open house, I note it. If it's shopping for groceries for that brokers' open house, I include that on the log. Each seller's log just keeps growing and growing.

As you go through your marketing program and your *Marketing Portfolio* with your sellers, commit to giving them an update report, expanded from that log, every two to six weeks, depending on the length of selling time in your area. If the market is hot promise a report every two weeks. If it's slow, promise a report every four to six weeks. It's just good business. Too many agents will list a property today and never really talk to the sellers again. Sellers deserve a lot more than that. They really appreciate receiving a typed report on the work you have done. This is one way I keep all my listings. The market could be good, or poor, but I can still keep my sellers happy. It is difficult for them to refute the work that has been done when they see a typed, detailed report. Be sure to take it to them when you present it. Do not go over it on the phone. Take it to them and go over it in person. It's the best kind of professional communication there is. (We will look at the actual form I use in the next chapter. It is also shown in the back of this book with other forms for your reference.)

Show sellers samples of a log and the reports you do for your sellers. This way they will fully understand the importance of the concept, and they will really appreciate the professional service.

FORMS THAT ARE USED IN THE SALE AND CLOSING

In this section of your *Marketing Portfolio* show copies of the purchase and sale agreement the multiple listing service uses in your area. If your company uses its own form, display it instead. Here, you can take the time to talk about the paperwork for the purchase and sale agreement. This takes care of some of the sellers' fears ahead of time. Remember, the time you spend now can head off problems later.

You can also include copies of a local lender's financing rate sheet, title insurance information, sample inspection report, sample appraisal report, or a blank deed form. Let them hold and touch these forms. Let them look at the small print on the front and back to get used to seeing it. This is a good time to share your experience and expertise in these areas.

I've also written down the steps of what it takes to close a transaction. I call this "steps to close a sale." I always take all the time it takes to go over this with my sellers so that they know how I will be involved every step of the way on their behalf until the successful culmination of their sale. I also always go with every seller to the closing. In some areas this is not a standard practice, but I believe it is an important last contact— both professionally and for future referral business. Why miss the closing when this is the moment we all have been working for? In my opinion it is like missing the "birthday" of the sale. Go— it is also a great time to ask that seller or buyer to write you a letter of recommendation about the great job you have just completed, which gives you another addition for your *Career Book*.

A powerful way to end your *Marketing Portfolio* is just as you did with your *Career Book*: a photo of you with a "SOLD" sign. I recommend that you have a photo taken of you in front of a home holding a sold sign by your company's sign. Remember we are selling *you* here, and if you don't sell you, then who will? Sellers are looking for an agent who knows how to market. They also know that the first thing you should market is you...to them. Have someone in your office take a photo of you and then put it in your *Marketing Portfolio* as a great close to your marketing program.

EDUCATION OF SELLERS TODAY!

By using a marketing presentation book, it just makes it so much easier for you to talk to sellers. Not only do they hear what you're talking about, they also see the fantastic work you do. Once you've used it, you won't want to give a presentation without it. Now you have the information you need to build one of the most powerful selling tools you will ever use. Put your *Marketing Portfolio* together now! Yours can be just the way you would like it. You tailor it to your own style. You put your own marketing techniques in it. You make it your own working tool. Use, enjoy, and be proud of your *Marketing Portfolio*. It will help you educate your sellers and get more listings. Do it now, because it really works!

When you put your listing presentation book together, you can use your company book and incorporate the ideas just mentioned above. Or, you could put samples of your marketing techniques into a visual sample book. My professionally designed *Marketing Portfolio* is available for you and is simple to use. All you have to do is slip your own work into the plastic sheet protectors provided and then place them behind the title pages. You then have your own custom-made marketing presentation book, with an easel-back cover designed to stand up by itself presentations. It is totally professional in representing you because *you* customize it with your work. Because you put it together yourself it will be totally personalized so it won't end up sitting on a shelf.

For details on ordering Barb's *Marketing Portfolio* please turn to the Appendix of this book.

8

Part One of Your Detailed Report: Exclusive Marketing Program

In this chapter you will learn

1. How to present your Marketing Program.
2. How your Marketing Program and your *Marketing Portfolio* work together to make a "show-and-tell" presentation.
3. In what areas to educate your sellers.
4. What are the "secrets of my success."

The key to sales is marketing. This chapter shows you how to use your Exclusive Marketing Program for the sale of the sellers' home in your listing presentation.

Before we begin let's do a quick review of the ideas, tools, and timing for their use, which I have introduced to this point.

1. The *Career Book* is to be left with the seller the first time you meet to sell you and your credibility. It is *not* a listing presentation book. It is a marketing book about *you.* Leave it and pick it up when you return to give your listing presentation, or the Detailed Report. (By the way, you simply cannot have too many *Career Books!*)

2. The *Marketing Portfolio* is your listing presentation book that you use to show samples of the work you will be doing to market and sell a home. You *never* leave it, and you only need one *Marketing Portfolio.*

3. The Exclusive Marketing Program is what you give sellers in writing to tell them what you will do to sell their home. This is included in your listing packet for each individual seller. It simply backs up in writing what you are showing them in your *Marketing Portfolio* as you go through the samples of all of your work during your listing presentation.

You always use the Exclusive Marketing Program at the same time you use the *Marketing Portfolio.* They feed each other and support each other totally as I will explain in this chapter.

EDUCATION! EDUCATION!

I know agents who have been in business for a long or even a short time who do *not* use a written marketing program or a listing presentation book. They always seem to stay at the same level of production— never reaching the top level of production they want, yet always complaining about why their production isn't increasing.

I strongly believe it is because they have not taken the time nor have they used the necessary tools to educate their sellers as to what techniques will be used to sell their home. If you will take the time to educate your sellers in the beginning, through a strong and powerful listing presentation, you will gain professional control, and you will start building a listing empire. As I have already pointed out, however, this cannot be accomplished in fifteen minutes. A good listing presentation should last at least an hour and a half to two hours.

Sellers today are very smart. The public is better educated than ever. They want to know what they are paying for in this day and age. And they deserve to know. I have heard sellers ask repeatedly, "What are you going to do to market and sell my house?" I have even seen sellers give out a list of demands to agents they interviewed.

These lists have included the following questions:

- What services do you offer?
- What is your range of fees?
- What is your success record?
- How long does it take for your listings to sell?
- What is your recommendation of selling price?
- What are the asking prices of nearby homes currently for sale?
- What is the written Competitive Market Analysis of recent selling prices of neighborhood homes?
- Can you supply three references of sellers you have worked with recently?

These are all reasonable requests. They want to know, and they have a right to know. Using the program I have developed you will be totally prepared ahead of time. You will be on the offense, not the defense!

Therefore, your second visit with your potential sellers is crucial. This is when you sit down with your sellers and present your Exclusive Marketing Program and your Comparative Market Analysis (discussed in a future chapter). In other words, you give the sellers an expanded version of "Let me tell you how I work." But you are not only educating your sellers with your listing presentation, you are also selling yourself by showing the marketing that you will commit to doing at this point. I really believe that service is the name of the game.

In this chapter, I will take you step-by-step through the first part of the second visit— the Exclusive Marketing Program, which you should tailor to suit each potential seller. My marketing presentation includes a listing packet, which I prepare specifically for each seller, that has my Exclusive Marketing Program and the Comparative Market Analysis in it. I then use my *Marketing Portfolio* as I have just described in the previous chapter to show them the examples of my work. The work that I am promising to do, in writing, is in the packet containing my Exclusive Marketing Program for the sale of their home.

PRESENTATION OF EXCLUSIVE MARKETING PROGRAM

I want to be sure you understand that giving the Detailed Report is really a show-and-tell presentation. How? Well, the Exclusive Marketing Program *tells* sellers what you will do to sell their home and the *Marketing Portfolio shows* them what you will do (discussed in the last chapter). I would never use one without the other. Tell them what you are going to do, and then show them a sample of your work.

For example, tell the sellers, as they look at your Exclusive Marketing Program, that you will prepare a flyer about their home for the multiple. Explain how they work, then show them a sample of flyers that you have done for other sellers in your *Marketing Portfolio*. Tell and show. Show and tell. This is how people learn. It is a proven fact!

Be sure to set up your *Marketing Portfolio* in front of the sellers as you begin your presentation. As you go through your presentation, you can show your sellers exactly what you are talking about and are going to do. Your words have much more impact when the sellers both see and hear what you are saying.

Studies show that if you tell people something, they will remember 60 percent of what you said for up to three hours and only 10 percent of it three days later (Figure 8-1). If you simply show people something, they still don't remember more than 62 percent of it three hours later; they remember only 18 percent of what you told them three days later. But if you combine both verbal and visual information, most people will remember 85 percent of what they saw and heard for a lengthy period of time. That's true education!

So, by using your *Marketing Portfolio* with your Exclusive Marketing Program, you increase your sellers' long-term memory

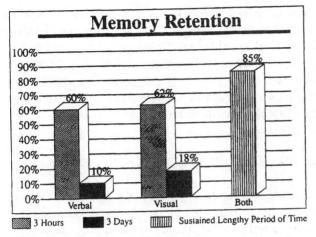

FIGURE 8–1 Memory Retention

retention by 65 percent to 75 percent! Also, a visual aid helps your sellers concentrate on your presentation.

As I go through this chapter on marketing with you, remember that as I promise the sellers a certain marketing technique, I show them that same technique in my *Marketing Portfolio*. In fact I wrote the marketing program and the *Marketing Portfolio* to go totally together. Tell and show. Tell and show.

As you begin your presentation, you can say something like, "Sally and John, as you can see, this is my Exclusive Marketing Program for the sale of your home. These are the commitments I make to you. As you'll see when we finish, I've signed my name to my Marketing Program to guarantee these commitments to you. It is my guarantee to you in writing as to what I will do to market and sell your home." (By the way, be sure you check this ahead of time. You don't want to turn to the last page and find you haven't signed your name.)

Explain to the sellers before you begin that the Marketing Program has been specifically designed for them. Tell them that you will leave the entire packet with them as soon as you begin to work together as a seller-and-agent team.

I feel very strongly that you should not leave your listing packet with sellers until they have signed the dotted line on the bottom of the listing agreement. Hours of your hard work go into that packet, and until you have a written commitment from the sellers to list with you, I don't think you should leave it with them. It's too easy for another agent with another company to come through, see your presentation lying on the kitchen counter and ask that seller, "Sally, do you mind if I look at that packet? I'll return it to you tomorrow." The seller is put in the middle. She doesn't know what to say, and it really doesn't make much difference to her if someone else does look at it. All your hard work ends up going out the door with another agent. I know because that happened to me once. All you have to do if a seller ever wonders why you won't leave it is to say that you have made it one of your professional policies. It is simply the way that you work. They will respect you once again...for your policies. Tell them that you give your packets to your sellers as they give you their commitment in writing. Tell them in the beginning of your presentation, before you start to go through it. By the way, I got more listings after I made this my policy, not less.

As you go through your presentation, you do not literally have to read all of the points on your program. Instead, use your Exclusive Marketing Program to trigger thoughts in your mind. Once again, you are going to tell your potential sellers how you work. Before you begin your presentation, explain to the sellers how you will divide the presentation into two parts: the Exclusive Marketing Program and your Comparative Market Analysis.

The following is a chronological breakdown of my Exclusive Marketing Program presentation. Adapt it to your style and any differences you may have in the area where you work.

EXCLUSIVE MARKETING PROGRAM

Introduction of Your Company

This is the time to discuss and provide information about your company: its history, its successes or awards, the services available, and the people who work there. You might spend ten to fifteen minutes or longer talking about your company with your sellers.

Listing Process

At this point in your *Marketing Portfolio* you should have a copy of the listing agreement. Tell the sellers as soon as you start to work together as a seller-and-agent team you will complete the paperwork (listing agreement) to bring them on the market. I also recommend that you review the listing agreement in detail with them at that time. Do take the time to answer any questions that they have now about the paperwork so that they understand anything they might be concerned about now. This can really help remove any fear factors about the listing agreement form.

As you start to discuss the listing process with your future sellers, tell them that you have prepared a Comparative Market Analysis, which you will be going over together with them in the second part of this presentation. This is a good time to say something like, "I feel that setting the price on your home is your ultimate decision. It is your home. But it is my job, as your future agent, to give you my honest, professional opinion of where I see us fitting in today's market in price and terms." Let them know that after you give them the analysis, you will work with them to determine the best possible list price for their home in today's market.

Preparation of Home for Sale

In discussing this important area I suggest that you tell your sellers that as you go to work together as "a seller-and-agent team" you will spend as much time as necessary going over their entire property with them, both inside and outside, to get the property ready to sell. Explain that you will make a list, with them, of suggestions and recommendations which will allow them to show their home at its very best. But put their minds at ease right away that this does not usually mean they have to spend a lot of money. All it usually takes is a little extra time and energy on their part. Stress to the sellers that this can be a lot of fun. And it really can be!

Teach your future sellers that this process is called *Staging*, which means preparing their home for sale. This is the best way for them to get the most amount of equity in the shortest amount of time. I haven't met a seller yet that wasn't really pleased by my recommendations. Refer to the before and after photos in your *Marketing Portfolio*, as we discussed in the last chapter, so they fully understand your service. Going over this with them is very important. If they have any concerns or questions, bring them up now and handle them. This way, there aren't going to be any problems for you when the time comes to *Stage* their home. Be up front about all of this, and your sellers will understand why it is so important. You don't do the work with them at this point, but you do want to explain why it is so important for them to prepare their home for sale. It will really pay off for you both when you come on the market together.

Explain to your sellers that what you are going to do is to pack them up early. If they are motivated sellers (and that is the key— motivated), you're not going to have any problems.

"With me as your agent, you are going to be moving, so, we're just going to pack you up a little bit early."

"For Sale" Sign and Access to Property

Another main issue to settle up front is the fact that you need to install a key box (key safe or lockbox) and a "For Sale" sign on their property. I always work to get the sellers to allow access to the property through a key box, and to have a sign. If you are not in an area where you have key boxes, then, of course, you are not going to be talking to the sellers about this. But I do believe in "For Sale" signs and key boxes to give as much exposure as possible. If you have other ways of accessing the property, be sure they conform with whatever most sellers do. If 99 percent of the other sellers out there allow access to their property one way, and the sellers you're working with say, "no," you have a problem. Tell them, "If you are totally different from the rest of the properties on the market, your property is just not going to be shown." It is important that you be honest with them and educate them about what is done in your own area.

I once was called by sellers to list an expensive property where the they would not have a key box or sign, the only time the house could be shown was Saturday mornings, and their daughter had to come with me to show the property. I told them that if they expected to get the property sold with me as their agent, they would have to have a key box and a "For Sale" sign, and they could not limit showings. I explained that everything they wanted to do would severely limit showings, and it could take ten times as long to find the right purchaser. Before I took the listing they finally did agree to follow my recommendations, but I was prepared to pass up the listing rather than to take on a property I knew I couldn't sell. So, take time to really educate your sellers. That couple was motivated to sell, and that is why educating them worked. If they weren't, educating them would not have made much difference.

Information Sheets

The next items in my Exclusive Marketing Program are information sheets. I always create a professional information sheet highlighting the key selling points of the sellers' home for prospective purchasers. At this point, I show the sellers samples of my information sheets in my *Marketing Portfolio*. I believe it is a good investment to have printed forms that look very professional.

Tell the sellers you would like to set up an information center in their house, preferably on the dining room table. Here you will place a stack of information sheets, and keep it supplied at all times for buyers and agents coming through their home. Ask the sellers to put out a little saucer for the cards of agents who show their home. Then, you can pick up the cards every Monday, or whatever day you plan, each week.

Information sheets give the showing agents all the "ammunition" they need to help sell the property. Prepare information sheets for each of your sellers. They deserve to be represented in the most professional way possible, and they will hire you as their agent because of it.

Figure 8–2 is a sample of the type of information sheet I have used.

Marketing Booklet

I prepare a separate marketing booklet for each of my sellers which remains in their home at all times. It is a collection of valuable information about my listings that I put together in a report-type folder. This is placed on the same table as the information sheets and is used for reference by the showing agent and purchaser as they look at the property. This is a great

---

THE (Seller's Name) RESIDENCE

OFFERED AT $

ADDRESS:

AREA:

AGE:

STYLE:

SQUARE FOOTAGE:

BEDROOMS:

BATHS:

BASEMENT:

GARAGE:

LOT SIZE:

PROPERTY TAXES:

TERMS:

LENDER INFORMATION:

UNIQUE FEATURES:

FIGURE 8–2 Sample Information Sheet

place to put shopping information, school information, athletic club information, park information, and so forth. Anything and everything that can help sell your listing can go in the booklet. I always put a lot of color pictures in it, no matter what the price of the property is— whether it is $100,000 or $1,000,000. I also include plat maps, loan information, and other pieces of information about the property. Providing all that information makes it easier for a buyer to make a decision. The marketing booklet should continue to grow as you market the property. As you do flyers or letters, or any type of marketing for the property, add it to the marketing booklet, so it will help agents when they come through the house. I prepare a booklet for each and every seller because the multiple does not have room for a lot of extra information, and this is the place I developed to put it.

Show your potential sellers the sample marketing booklet you have prepared, as explained earlier, and placed in your *Marketing Portfolio*, and tell them they will have their own individual marketing booklet. I always try to have the title page typed for their future book before I go to see them and slip it onto the cover of my sample one in my *Marketing Portfolio*. I also secure the property records from the title company ahead of time and insert those as well. All this makes for an impressive presumptive close. Sellers look at the beginning of their book, and say, "Oh, isn't that great, Barb has started ours already." I am assuming, and I want them to assume, that I am going to be their agent. I've already started working for them by preparing this booklet.

On the booklet it says, "Please Do Not Remove." I've only had two taken in ten years, and all I did was to quickly make up another one from the copies of everything I had in my file back at the office. I also strongly suggest that you put in a disclaimer about the information in the booklet. I have never had a legal problem of any kind. I believe that is because I am always thinking ahead of time about what could arise and working to prevent it. I wouldn't want to put something in the booklet that I got from the county records and then later on find out the county was wrong. Therefore, consult your company attorney or manager regarding the exact wording, but it is wise to place the burden of responsibility on the purchaser to verify all information contained in the booklet, prior to close of the sale. Have them sign this page at the time the house or property is sold for the protection of both you and your sellers.

SECRETS OF MY SUCCESS

The next area I cover with potential sellers I call the "secrets of my success." We will go into even more detail on each of these marketing ideas in the next chapter. For now, I am going to list them in much the same way I present them to sellers.

Company Tour

I personally conduct a tour of the sellers' home for all the sales agents in my office. I explain to potential sellers that I personally bring all the agents from my office to see my sellers' homes. This occurs on the first office meeting as soon as the property has been prepared for sale.

Multiple Listing Association

I professionally represent all my homes in the multiple listing book for my area, and I want potential sellers to know this. As a result, my homes are exposed to every agent in the area. At this point in the presentation, I show my sellers my *Marketing Portfolio*, which has maps of the areas included in our multiple listing association. (This also helps educate sellers to the areas that you will be showing them comparables from in the second part of your report.) Next show off the pages from your multiple book in your *Marketing Portfolio* to your sellers so they can see exactly how it will look when their house comes on the market (as discussed in the last chapter). I like to show them a page that has one or more of my listings on it. Again, this is all part of the education program I include in my listing presentation, and many agents don't take the time to do this. Take the time to show the sellers that you go a step farther than most other agents. Then they can really appreciate your work. Take the time to explain what you are showing them about the multiple. Remember, if *you* don't sell you, no one else will!

Brokers' Open Houses

I also explain to sellers how I work in a brokers' open house. I show them the information in my *Marketing Portfolio* as I cover this area. Again, I want them to know they are getting service a cut above the average. I will promise my sellers a certain number of brokers' open houses. I would never commit to more than I could handle, but I will commit to more than most other agents in the area. Teach the sellers that in this way you will be reaching many more purchasers through the agents that will be attending the brokers' open houses you will be holding.

Flyers

Here, I show my sellers samples in my *Marketing Portfolio* of the flyers I have produced, and I make a commitment to do the same thing to market their property in my Exclusive Marketing Program. I point out to sellers how professional my flyers really do look. Sellers don't know what you don't tell them. They really need to see the quality of your work.

I remember giving a presentation to a seller and just telling him I would prepare a flyer and he said, "What's a flyer?" I realized because he was, of course, in another line of work that he did not understand what a flyer was. Therefore, I started to bring samples of my flyers along with me (and other marketing techniques as well) so that the sellers could not only hear what I would be doing to sell their homes, but so they could *see* what I would be doing and how I worked.

Exclusive Agent Mailing List

Sellers are fascinated by this list. Show them the lists of names or pages of business cards you have in your *Marketing Portfolio* and how you developed your mailing list (discussed in the last chapter). Tell them what an effective marketing tool this is, as agents watch for your mailings. Describe also how you will market their home through your exclusive agent mailing list. Show them one of your past mailings.

For example, I always say to my sellers during the presentation, "When I call you to say I have a mailing of the top 450 agents at the post office ready to go out tonight, then I want you to know that as one of my listings I am doing this on your behalf." It takes a lot of time and energy to have the mailer printed, duplicated, folded, labeled, stapled, addressed, stamped, and mailed, but it is worth it! I find that every time I do a mailing, almost without exception, a purchase and sale agreement will come in on one of my listings.

Annual Letter to the Agents

Show them the letter in your *Marketing Portfolio* that you send to the agents on your exclusive mailing list at the beginning of each new year. This is very impressive.

Agent Rapport

Explain to potential sellers the value of motivating agents to show and sell their home. Let them know this is a part of your marketing strategy. Tell them about the special way you treat other agents you work with at your own company and at all the other companies in the area.

Advertising

Tell your sellers about the advertising your company does and any advertising you do personally. Explain exactly how you advertise homes and property for sale— where, when, how regularly, and so forth. Show them the samples of your advertisements from newspapers or magazines in your *Marketing Portfolio.*

At this point, you want to teach sellers that ads don't sell homes— agents do. That's the truth. Ads do two things: They make the company telephone ring, and they bring purchasers into the company. They also make sellers feel good, because they see their home in the paper and feel good that the company has advertised the property. But during all my years of real estate, I have observed that most houses are sold by agents bringing qualified purchasers to show the home and then selling it. So it is really important to teach your sellers how ads actually work.

Public Open Houses

Educate potential sellers as to the value of public open houses. As the professional agent, I believe it is up to you to determine how many open houses you recommend holding for the seller and when you recommend holding them. Many times this is based, of course, on where the house is located. In this way, you stay in control by teaching your sellers how open houses really work.

Communication with Sellers

The next step in your presentation is to make a commitment to your potential sellers to maintain regular communications with them. Tell them that when you begin to work together, you will continue to communicate directly with them about your marketing and the progress toward the sale of their home as well as the conditions of the current market.

Let them know, however, that a lot of your work is behind the scenes. You might even say, "Mr. and Mrs. Seller, you won't see me as much physically when I am marketing your home, because a lot of my work is in the marketplace; however, I will be talking with you every week as my work for you progresses. I think that is so important. I want to call you before you call me. I want you to know, week by week, what I am doing to market your home; who is calling about your home; what they are saying; what some of the feedback is from showings; and what some of the purchasers are saying."

In addition to weekly phone conversations, make a commitment to potential sellers to give them update reports at specific intervals to let them know exactly what you are doing to market their home. I find that sellers appreciate this commitment. This can give you a real edge on your competition and get you the listing because most other agents will not promise this to sellers or haven't even thought of doing it. In your Exclusive Marketing Program you can write, "Sally and John, I will provide a written report every four to six weeks to inform you fully of all my work and all the marketing done on your behalf to that date." Sellers love this promise!

Turn to your *Marketing Portfolio* and explain the report to your sellers. Show them the sample of an update report you did for other sellers. Show your sellers the log you have already started for them with your first visit, and explain you will keep a log for everything you do to market their home. I don't lose listings, and one reason for that is that I keep my sellers posted as to the progress of the marketing I do for them.

Figure 8–3 is a sample of the form for the marketing update report.

Barb's Marketing
Update Report

For

It is my sincere pleasure to be representing you as your listing and marketing agent in the sale of your home. Below is listed some of the work that I have completed to date for you, as we work together towards a successful completion of our goal.

(Your report by date goes here)

Samples i.e.

June 10th — Held Broker's Open from 10:00 to 1:00. I served refreshments to the agents. Comments were good with 18 agents attending.

June 14th — An ad was run in The Seattle Times in the Open House section for Sunday. I held open house from 2:00 to 5:00 P.M. and had a low turn-out. There was one couple looking in a lower price range and a single person looking for decorating ideas.

June 18 — Worked on a creative flyer for 3 hours in the afternoon promoting your home. This will be published and distributed to 2,000 agents next week in our multiple.

I hope you are pleased with the above work that I have completed to this date for you. I shall continue my work and dedication as we progress towards a completed sale of your home. Thank you.

Most sincerely,

(Your Name)
(Your Title)
(Your Company)

© 1986 Barb Schwarz

FIGURE 8-3   Sample Marketing Update Report

Sale and Handling of Details

This category really excites sellers, because now you are talking about their goal...to sell their house. Here, show potential sellers copies of the purchase and sale agreement the multiple listing association uses in your area. Also show them information such as your local lender's financing rate sheet, title insurance information, a sample inspection report, etc. Let them get involved in your presentation as this is the goal they have for selling— to be sold!

Explain to your sellers that you want to be present at any and all purchase and sale agreement presentations, which is really important. Multiple rules vary from association to association or from area to area, so this may be different for you. In my multiple both listing and selling agents traditionally are present at the presentation of an offer. However, as the listing agent I would not ever want any sellers of mine to sit down by themselves with the selling agent, without me, because how could I represent them without being there?

So, what should your sellers do if the selling agent with the offer calls them directly and says, "Mr. and Mrs. Seller, I'm so excited: I've got a purchase and sale agreement on your property, and I want to come over right now and present it". Sellers are really tempted to let them. They are excited to see it because they want to sell the house. But ask your sellers to say a few simple words to that other agent: "Have you talked to my listing agent, yet?" If he says, "No, I haven't been able to get her (or him)," ask your seller to reply to that other agent, "When we can reach our listing agent, and she (or he) can be here for the presentation, then we'll be glad to look at it. If it is tonight, great. If it is tomorrow, great. But we must have our listing agent here."

Now is the perfect time to educate your sellers on why it is so important for you to be present at any and all purchase and sale agreement presentations. Give your sellers alternate numbers to call in case you are out of town. For example, my sellers have my broker's number and the number of the owner of the company where I work. None of my sellers has ever been alone when an agreement was presented. It's just too important. Explain to sellers that once they sign that agreement, that's the way it is. If a seller or a purchaser decides to make a change, both of them have to agree to that change. It is a legal document. A "war story" of your own or one you have heard at this point can really drive the point home so that they will really want your expertise there with them at the presentation of any offer.

Qualifying Buyers

Tell sellers that qualifying purchasers is a part of closing a sale smoothly. Tell them you will do your very best to help in the qualifying of potential purchasers who are interested in their home. This is true whether it is someone you may have shown, someone another agent from your office has shown, or someone a salesperson from another company in town has shown. Qualifying buyers as much as possible ahead of time is crucial to the close of the sale.

Also at this point, I suggest you tell sellers something that will probably shock them. Tell them it will probably shock them, but then they will understand. Tell them you probably won't be the agent who sells their home. Tell them even your own office or company may not even sell their home. But, add that by the time you get through doing all the work you are going to do, they will say, "You sold our home," because you work so hard to reach all the possible agents who work with potential purchasers for their property. Tell them this is your job...to reach as many other salespeople with potential purchasers as possible. You might even tell your sellers they probably won't even remember who that other agent was who brought in the purchaser. They won't remember because you did all the work to get them there.

Teach them that the person they hire to market their property is entirely different from the person who may actually bring the buyer through their front door. There is a *big* difference between the selling agent and the listing agent because the listing agent is really their *marketing expert*. Who they hire as this *marketing expert* will totally determine how many buyers see their home and how quickly buyers will respond to the marketing. Tell them you want to be the *marketing expert*, the one who encourages agents from all the different companies in town to bring their buyers through the sellers' home. If you tell them this now, you won't hear this complaint later: "You never showed the house. How come you've never brought a purchaser to see our home?" Or, "What's going on down at your company? No one from your company ever shows our house." When I heard that objection for the first time I thought to myself, "Well, I know why that is. It's because there are a lot of companies and agents out there, and the statistics in the multiple show that more homes are sold by other companies than the listing company."

But the sellers won't know this if you don't tell them. So, educate your sellers up front. Show them the multiple statistics. Include them in your presentation. You can choose from several different spots. I add it here, because I am thinking about the other agent who might be bringing in another purchaser, who I will need to help qualify.

Financing

Keep abreast of all the current financing programs available, so you can help purchasers find the best financing possible today. This is another extra service that will set you apart from most other listing agents, so let potential sellers know this is a special service. During your presentation, show sellers the sample finance sheet in your *Marketing Portfolio.*

Even when another agent brings in a purchaser, I work with that agent, for my sellers, in securing the financing for the buyer. This practice goes a long way in building agent rapport, and it sometimes speeds up the sale. So, work with the mortgage companies in your area to find the best companies and their representatives, whether you are the listing or selling agent. You can help closings go more smoothly.

Closing the Sale

Now you are at the most crucial step. What you tell potential sellers at this point in your presentation makes a big difference in whether or not you get the listing. So, explain to your sellers that you work extremely hard in this area, and then do it!

If you have done all the work to represent your sellers, and you don't get the sale closed, then all that work has been for nothing. Tell potential sellers, "I will do whatever it takes— as long as it moral, ethical, and legal— to get the sale closed for you." I really believe in this philosophy. I have driven three hours to other cities to deliver papers at midnight because a bank forgot to have a purchaser sign three additional documents. I then turned around and at half past two in the morning drove to another city to deliver them to the escrow officer at her own home. The sale closed on time, and that is the only way it would have closed on time. Whatever it takes, as long as it is legal, moral, and ethical, get it done.

You must watch after everyone involved in a sale: the banker, attorney, appraiser, escrow people, and inspectors. Watch and follow the transaction to be sure it closes.

Tell potential sellers you will keep them informed continually as to the progress of their transaction from the time of the signing until the closing of the sale (in some areas of the country this is called settlement). Tell them that in the escrow and closing area, you will work hard to handle any situations that may arise with the mortgage bankers, escrow agents, appraisers, underwriters, inspectors, purchasers, and other agents up to the actual close of the sale.

Last but not least, let your sellers know you will go with them, if they would like, to the signing of the closing documents at the close of the sale. I suggest you do that because many times I've seen such things as an extra, unexplained fee come up at the very end. Someone had better be there to solve the situation. I remember a closing that I went to that had a wrong fee on it. The seller said, "What is this? I am not signing these papers at all." The escrow officer said, "Well this fee is one the mortgage company is charging." I said, "That fee is not supposed to be there." If I hadn't been there, no one really would have known. We could have been delayed two, three, or even five days. But, because I was there, I was able to get on the phone, track down the particular loan representative, and handle the situation. And the sale closed on time.

Tell your sellers stories like the one I just shared with you so that they know the extent of how hard you work for them.

ENDING OF MARKETING PRESENTATION

"SOLD" Sign

As I stated in the last chapter, a photo of you holding a "SOLD" sign in front of your company sign with a home in the background is a great way to end your presentation with your *Marketing Portfolio*. It has impact and gives a great final emphasis to your whole marketing program as you've presented it to your sellers.

Major Commitment

Explain to potential sellers that your Exclusive Marketing Program is your commitment to them. You can say something like, "I will work hard to represent you in the prompt sale of your home at the very best possible price. I receive payment for my services when, and only when, you have received the proceeds from the sale of your home. And I look forward to serving you." Then you close your listing packet, but keep your *Marketing Portfolio* open at the same time to your "SOLD" photo, and just reiterate, "This is my commitment to you."

Once you have presented all that you plan to do to market the sellers' property, you can wrap up the marketing presentation by going over other information you may have in their packet, in the marketing section. This is the time to show them information about their specific property: the title records from the county, the taxes, their plat map, and any information the assessor from the county has on this particular piece of property, such as the lot size, square footage, the year built, and so forth. Add all these things in the back of your listing packet, which you will eventually leave with the sellers once they have signed the listing agreement. Make sure all your information is correct. And don't forget to ask potential sellers to sign a request for verification of loan information about their current loan from their bank or mortgage company. (See sample loan information letter at the back of the book in the form section.) You need their signature to get the information about the financing on their present home in writing from their lending institution. You want to know all of the facts about their current loan as soon as possible as the listing agent. This is just a good, safe practice to do. It keeps unpleasant surprises from springing up later on at the sale or the close of the sale. A good thing about asking for the signature at this time is that if your seller says, "OK, let's go ahead and sign it," you can be fairly sure you have the listing! If they are not ready to sign the loan information letter yet, that's all right, just proceed with the rest of your presentation. They can authorize it when you fill out the listing agreement later.

MASTER YOUR MARKETING PROGRAM

Now, as you can see, this is a powerful marketing program. This is because you have taken the time to really educate your potential sellers as to how you work. It does take time to educate, but if you will do this up front it really means fewer problems and objections later. I have yet to find a seller who didn't love it. It covers the sale of a home from the beginning when you both sign the listing agreement all the way to the close of the sale. There are stories you can share in each area— either ones I have told you or stories of your own.

Use the *Marketing Portfolio* I have designed for you to put together your own program, and it will flow right along with you as you cover your Exclusive Marketing Program with your sellers. They flow together and reinforce each other. Show and tell. Tell and show. Together they are strong and powerful. I spend probably an hour going over all of the marketing with potential sellers. Adapt it to serve you and your company, using your own style. Your Exclusive Marketing Program sets the *Stage* for the second part of Step 2— your Comparative Market Analysis.

9

Power Behind
the Secrets of My
Success

In this chapter you will learn

1. The secrets of successful marketing.
2. How the marketing techniques work together as a total marketing plan.
3. How to add even more power to some of the "secrets of my success."

The beauty of my Exclusive Marketing Program is that each marketing tool works well alone. When you use them together, however, you have a truly powerful package. Use these tested and proven techniques, and you will list more homes and reach more purchasers than you ever have before.

In the last chapter I discussed educating your sellers up front about marketing—especially in regard to the secrets of success. In this chapter I will go into detail about the work to do behind the scenes to add even more strength and power to those secrets of success.

Not only will these techniques help you sell more of your listings, but when you present these techniques to your future sellers, they will list with you! These techniques can help you get more listings, then you can use them to make more sales, no matter what the market is doing.

SECRETS OF SUCCESSFUL MARKETING

Company Tour

All of the agents from your office should always tour each others' listings. Not some agents some weeks and some the next. But all of the agents, all of the time.

Give the agents from your office a personal tour of all your listed homes. This also shows total office support to your sellers as the company tours their home. This way the other agents in your firm always know your properties firsthand, and they will be prepared when they answer ad calls or sign calls regarding the homes you have listed. Or they may come across a purchaser who is looking for what you have. So, familiarize them with your homes. Insist on it. A good time for the tour is the first Monday or Tuesday after you put the house on the market, but only after the sellers have completely prepared their home for sale. Remember, "agents only know what they see, not the way it's going to be."

Multiple Listing Association

If you professionally represent all your homes in the multiple listing book in your area, they are exposed to every agent in the area. As I have said before, most of my marketing targets other agents. The MLS book is a great way to enlist the selling power of all the agents in other companies in your area. That way, you reach as many purchasers as you possibly can. For this reason, I recommend you enter your listings in the MLS book with as much pizzazz as you can. Make your listings jump off the page. When other agents open the book, you want them to know which properties are yours.

If your MLS book has supplements (sometimes called addenda) buy one for each of your listings. It's the cheapest form of advertising there is. If your listings pop right off the page, other agents will be more likely to show your properties before they show others.

A great idea is to put in the remarks section, "this home has been *Staged.*" (but only if this is true). This way all of the agents who use my *Staging* ideas can know this home has been prepared for sale!

Brokers' Open Houses

Open houses for other brokers work! Really shine in this area. You can also use them as one of your most effective marketing tools. Hold brokers' open houses regularly for agents in the multiple in your area for each of your listings until they sell. My record for brokers' open houses on one property is seventeen. That's right! (It was during a very slow market, but I sold the home at a brokers' open house!) The reason for holding lots of brokers' open houses is because in many multiple areas, you have as many as two thousand working agents, or more. Now, let's say you hold a brokers' open house, and twenty-five agents attend. You may consider that brokers' open house a success. But what about the other 1,975 agents who didn't make it?

So, if you hold just one brokers' open house, as many agents do, then you've really sold that property short. You need to reach as many of those agents as you can. Hold brokers' open houses on each of your properties on a regular basis. It's a good idea to hold one each week of the first three weeks the property comes on the market. After that, put the property on a rotating schedule, such as once a month. Also, sellers will give you their listings when you promise more than one brokers' open house. Point out that many agents hold only one brokers' open house for a seller. That seller is being sold short on service.

Many agents say to me, "How can you hold all these brokers' open houses if you have thirty-five listings, or even if you have only ten or fifteen?" Well, you don't get all your listings on one night, right? Tonight, if you go to list a home, you are not going to list thirty-five more that same evening, or even five more. So, start plugging your listings onto your calendar on a rotating basis. Those that have been on the market the longest, just hold them open once a month. Those that have just come on, hold them open this week and once a week for the next two weeks. In my area, we hold open houses for other agents on Tuesday, Wednesday, Thursday, and Friday, so I don't have to worry about scheduling more than one house each day. Usually they are spread out over days and weeks. I find that when I have more than one house to hold open for a brokers' open house, I can get assistance from other agents in my office who don't list as much. I will take them to lunch in return or help them with something else. A trade works well when you work in the right office.

When you hold a brokers' open house, don't sit at the kitchen table and just let the agents saunter through the house. Greet them at the door, go through the house with them, and try to help them think of buyers who would be interested in that particular home. For example, I might meet an agent at the front door and say, "Mary, how are you? Come on in!" I would lead her through the house, and say, "Mary, I want to show you this house! I'm so excited to have this listing. I want to take you through this home, and I hope you'll have someone you can sell it to." Now, many times I will take an agent's hand, look him or her in the eye, and say, "Mary, who do you have that you could sell this home to?"

As agents, you and I know that we get into our cars, go on tours, and start plodding on the treadmill. Sometimes we forget to match purchasers with the homes we see on tour. But to sell, you have to do some matching. So, I stop whoever comes in the door, greet them, and often even give them hugs. In fact, a lot of agents come to see me just for their hugs. They say, "Barb, I came to get my hug, and then I'll see the house." I want them to feel good about themselves. I want them to feel good about me. I want them to feel good about real estate. I want them to feel good about the home that I am holding open. I've got to sell those agents on selling this home.

Now, when I ask Mary if she is working with a purchaser that would buy my listing, sometimes she'll say, "Barb, I don't think I know anybody I can sell this home to." And I say, "Now wait a minute. Mary, I want you to really think about it. Are you sure? Didn't you meet someone last week or the week before?" Mary might stop a second, look up at the ceiling and say, "Gee, Barb, I didn't think so, but..." She may look over at me and say, "but you know, maybe I did. I met a young couple a few weeks ago. It looks like the yard is not quite what they were looking for as far as the setting goes. But, if the rest of the house looks like this, I think maybe I could show it to them." I've had agents actually do this. They'll go make a call to the purchaser, show them the house and sell it! If I hadn't asked, the sale would never have happened.

Flyers

Flyers are wonderful! They carry so much impact. Have flyers for each of your properties professionally produced, and send at least one flyer about each of your properties to every agent in your multiple area. Use colored paper, and include a copy of the camera card with a picture of the property so the agents can see what you are selling. Because you send these flyers to agents, not purchasers, try to include all the information agents need to know, like price, square footage, terms, and so forth.

Remember your image can be partly based on how your flyers look. A flyer is not a piece of paper and some marks with a felt-tip pen. You are not only representing your sellers, but yourself, your company, and the quality of your work. So, take the time, money, and energy to do them right. It will really pay off for you in the long run.

Exclusive Agent Mailing List

I have already explained to you how to develop an agent mailing list. I can't stress enough how strong this tool is. I suggest that you waste no time in building your own exclusive agent mailing list, and put it in your *Marketing Portfolio*. With this mailing list you can reach as many of the top agents in your area as possible. Once you have those eye-catching flyers produced, you can go to your mailing list and start labeling. Think about the impact you have when you mail information about your listings to 50 of the top agents in your area. Or how about reaching the top 100, 200, or even 500? My mailing list has grown from 50 agents to more than 450! Those numbers represent a lot of agents who work with a lot of purchasers.

Try it! This is something you can do wherever you live, whatever multiple area you work in. Build a network. In this business, we butter each other's bread. I don't think we can stand in the corner and isolate ourselves. We need to open our listings to all the other agents out there, but especially to the top, hard-working, full-time agents. I would rather have another agent sell one of my listings— we both make money, and the sellers get their equity— than for me to take six months to sell the house all alone.

An agent mailing list works! Take advantage of this great idea. Start calling the real estate companies in your area today and put that list together *now*.

Annual Letter to Agents

This letter (discussed in a previous chapter) is magic, so make it a New Year's Day habit. The foundation of a good marketing strategy is strong name recognition. You want agents to remember you, to know you are still out there ready and willing to work with them. Use this letter to remind all the agents on your mailing list how effective it is for you to work together. You can send it out more than once a year, each time with a different theme. What I am asking you to do is to build a following of other real estate agents. It works whether you are brand new in the business or you have been in it for years. Too many established agents have been rude to other agents, have not returned their calls, and have a bad reputation in the multiple. Set yourself aside from that kind of reputation. All that kind of reputation does is hurt the agent who has it. Instead, build a reputation of friendliness, kindness, professionalism, and cooperation with all. It will repay you many times over, I promise.

Agent Rapport

There is more to working with agents than just making that first contact. You want to establish relationships with other agents. You want them to know who you are and to enjoy working with you. This helps you and your sellers.

This is all a part of my efforts to target other agents in my area and to reach their purchasers. I go out of my way to make their experiences with my listings pleasant ones. I have story after story about agents who have walked into my listings and said to my sellers, "You've got the best agent in town because she really tries to work for you and with us to get your property sold."

As I stated earlier many agents out there don't return phone calls or cooperate with other agents working with another company. I return phone calls to other agents because I know how important their work is. In fact, I will return a phone call to an agent just as fast or maybe even faster than I would return a seller's call. The agent might have a purchaser for one of my listings right then, and if I don't get the call returned, we may both lose a sale.

Kill 'em with kindness—say "thank you!"

I send a gift to the selling agent, the day the sale closes, every time an agent sells one of my listings. Even though it is just roses or a fruit basket, I cannot begin to tell you how much this means to that agent. I have many notes from agents who have written that no other agent has ever thanked them before. Write the selling agent a note and send a small gift to say "thank you for selling one of my listings." Those agents will be back again and again to sell your listings. I promise!

I believe you need to spend money to make money. In other words, be willing to invest some money on your behalf and your sellers' behalf. I created the following idea for agents during a month when we had a very slow market, which can happen anywhere, any time:

> **"Show and sell any one of my quality listings in the month of October, and I'll send you for a night on the town and a weekend for you and your spouse at the Westin Hotel."** [1]

Always ask yourself what you can do to create some extra interest and some extra showings of your listings. My idea turned out to be a great one, because a number of agents showed my listings, and three of the properties I had listed in the month of October sold! It was my pleasure to send those particular agents and their spouses for a dinner at one of our area's finest restaurants, and for a weekend at the Westin, on me.

So, work with the other agents. Treat them with respect, and make it as easy as possible for them to sell your listings. By doing these things agents will beat a path to your door to show and sell your listings repeatedly. You can take that to the bank!

Advertising

Advertise wherever and whenever possible, and get the most from the advertising you do. But, as I said in a previous chapter, you have to understand one thing, and you want to educate your sellers so they understand this, too: "Ads don't sell homes; agents do."

Now, I'm not discouraging you from advertising. I just think it is important for you and your sellers to know how advertising works. Psychologists tell us purchasers respond to advertisements to eliminate them from the list of homes they might be interested in seeing; they don't necessarily call to buy them.

Give your sellers an idea of how advertising works: Let's say your sellers' home is advertised this week in the newspaper in your area. Then for the next two to three weeks, another similar home is advertised. Companies advertise by price ranges, so

---

[1] Be sure this type of program is allowed by your multiple listing association. Generally, bonus or incentive programs among agents are accepted, but some regions do prohibit them. Check in your area before you make such an offer.

even when your sellers' home is not in the paper, you will still get calls. People will call on another property in a particular price range but may end up looking at your listing. In other words, you get showings from other agents' ads and listings. You could also say something like this to your sellers: "Mr. and Mrs. Seller, I've seen only a few homes sold because of the specific ad on that piece of property. But I've seen many homes sold from other ads for other properties." Therefore, I do not get complaints from sellers saying, "When in the world are we going to be advertised, Barb? You never run any ads...." Really educate your sellers ahead of time about the advertising program of your company. This will head off complaints before they come up.

Another way to head off complaints is to always notify your sellers when their property is going to be advertised. One advertiser I know estimates that nearly sixty percent of all sellers don't know their property has been advertised. Call them ahead of time and let them know. Then send them an announcement in the mail. It is also a good idea to keep a sample of the announcement in your *Marketing Portfolio*. The announcement can be simple. Just paste a copy of the advertisement to your company letterhead and, across the bottom, write:

> **"Just because we want you to know we are working hard to represent you on the sale of your home."**

Write the date of publication, and the name of the newspaper or magazine in which it appeared. Sellers like to know what you are doing to market their homes, and this is yet another way to keep them informed. So, every time one of your properties is advertised, call your sellers and send them an announcement. Also keep copies of all advertisements in your own files. Then, as you make your next listing presentation and outline your marketing program for your sellers, teach them that it's a combination of all the marketing techniques you use that will sell their home.

Public Open Houses

Public open houses can be a double-edged sword, regardless of whether you love or hate to hold them. It is a fact of life that open houses are important for selling homes. The key to an effective public open house is to hold the right house open at the right time. Holding public open houses with resale property is sometimes less productive than holding an open house for a builder in a given development or plat, unless the property is in a heavy-traffic area. Educate your resale sellers that holding their houses open Sunday after Sunday may not be the most productive marketing strategy. Of course, things are different in a city where there is not much new construction or especially if you are in a hot market.

Educate your sellers according to their particular situations. Let's say Sally and John's home is tucked away on a cul-de-sac at the back of a huge older development, and no one ever drives in there. It wouldn't be productive for you to sit there Sunday after Sunday holding the house open. Just explain, "Sally and John, I really feel that because of where your home is located, it is going to be sold by one of the other marketing techniques we've talked about, so I won't be holding regular public open houses for you. But I will be holding brokers' open houses, which is how I am going to reach the agents who are working with the purchasers."

Leave the door open for them, though, by adding, "Now, Sally and John, if we have been on the market for some time, and we have not yet secured a purchase and sale agreement, then we may need to take another look at holding your house open. But, first, I want to try my other techniques to market your home." Because you are educating your sellers, you won't get complaints about not holding enough open houses. They will understand why.

Now, let's say Sally and John live on the corner of an extremely busy street. They are in a prime location for reaching purchasers through an open house. Other agents in your office may want to hold that home open on a given Sunday or Saturday. You can say, "Sally and John, it should be productive to hold your house open. A lot of potential purchasers will come by this area, so the chances of reaching them with an open house are good."

Educate them so they are willing to have an open house. If they don't want it held open, talk to them about possibly holding the house open every other Sunday, or at least once a month. You might be able to sell it more quickly that way.

Think through the specific situation before you go for Step 2 to give your presentation. When you go to see the house for the first time, you can tell if it is a property you want to hold open as much as possible, if it is a property that agents from your office are going to want to hold open, or if it is a property that no one is going to want to hold open. Be prepared to educate your sellers in the direction you feel is most effective for marketing their home.

Communication with Seller

The written report for the sellers, as I discussed in the last chapter, is a technique that will give you many more listings. Many agents have a habit of keeping track of what they do for their sellers and that's great. The only problem is that it then goes into their drawers in their desk. If you have been logging everything you do for your sellers on the front of a folder and then putting it in your desk drawer at work, think about this. Your drawers are eating up your income many times. Get them out of your drawers. Take them to the sellers who pay you.

Sellers love getting the reports, in writing, from you. By showing prospective sellers in your listing presentation that you will prepare for them written reports, you will simply get more listings. An extra benefit that will make you more money is that now you won't lose listings should they expire. There will be no reason for you to lose them because the sellers cannot say you have not done the work. They will have it all in writing, in their hands, in the form of a typed report. Terrific! Do it. It works.

After you get the listing, when it is time, prepare their report and put down everything you have been doing to market and sell their home. This includes open houses, both brokers' and public; ads in magazines and newspapers; flyers you have prepared; agent mailings you have prepared and sent; special calls you have made to other agents and packets of information you have prepared about their home for other agents; the time you spent as you began working with the sellers, including the periods during Steps 1 to 3; and even time you have spent shopping for groceries if you gave and prepared a luncheon for a brokers' open house.

Double space your report if you like for extra mileage. Type it up but never send it to your sellers. Call up your sellers and tell them that you have their report and want to bring it over. Ask them if tomorrow at six or six thirty would be better? Then take it over at the agreed time and sit down with both sellers at the table where you have always sat. Then give it to your sellers to read. Give the original copy to the decision maker and a copy to the spouse. Ask them to read it right then. Don't talk until the sellers have finished reading it and start talking with you first. You will find that sellers really appreciate you and all of your work more than ever before. They forget many of the things you have done to market their home. That is why this works so well.

Now, if for some reason the property has not sold by the time the second report is due (this could be between two and eight weeks depending on the time frame you promised the sellers) type up a new report starting after the conclusion of the last one. Then gather the first and second reports together (they may have misplaced the first report), and once again go see your sellers to present the new report. Now you have the history of the marketing of the property for you and your sellers. This is where it should be...in the hands of your sellers and not just in your drawers. Be sure that you do keep your own copy of the report in the sellers' file at your office. Now, you have the perfect tool to ask for a price reduction. Also take along copies of all the marketing techniques you have used as well as information on what the market is now doing. Show your sellers what the newest competition is since you have come on the market together. Then show them what has expired and what has sold for what price. Take photos with you, not just computer readouts. Then all you have to really do is sum everything up— your marketing report, your marketing techniques, and a brand new Comparative Market Analysis. Then tell your sellers that as their professional agent it is your recommendation that it is time for a price reduction. You are now on the offense because of all of the information you have just presented. The strongest piece of information is your Marketing Update Report. Sellers may sit and discuss this with you a bit, I find, but time after time you will get the price reduction because they cannot say you have not done the work.

This is one of the most powerful ideas I have ever developed. I believe in it totally. It puts us on a more professional level in the sellers' eyes. I believe it is information that we owe to our sellers and ourselves to share!

SYNERGY!

Now that you have more detailed descriptions of each of these secrets, the real secret to successful marketing is to use all of them together. Individually, the components are powerful. But, when you mix them together, it's explosive! So, take each technique, adapt it to your style and situation, and use all of them as a total marketing strategy. You will get more listings from sellers, reach more purchasers, and sell and close more listings.

10

Part Two of the Detailed Report: Comparative Market Analysis

In this chapter you will learn

1. The importance of a Comparative Market Analysis.
2. How to develop a Comparative Market Analysis for each of your sellers.
3. How to get the most impact from your comparables.

Sometimes sellers want to reject our professional opinion when we suggest a list price on their home. They will be much more cooperative, I believe, if they see how they fit into today's market in their area. A Comparative Market Analysis helps them understand how to determine the right list price for their home.

UNDERSTANDING EQUALS COOPERATION

Setting the price for a seller's home can sometimes be the toughest part of your listing presentation. Most sellers are proud of their homes, and even when they are really ready to sell they can be pretty emotional, especially concerning price. Unfortunately, a home, like anything else, is only worth what someone else is willing to pay for it. So, regardless of how valuable a seller believes his or her home is, you and I both know a house that is seriously overpriced is not going to sell.

I would not consider making a Detailed Report (listing presentation) without explaining my Comparative Market Analysis to my potential sellers. The beauty of this analysis is that you can show your sellers, on paper, exactly how you arrived at the suggested list price for their home. I don't show them the price until we have looked at all of the pricing information. Sellers are much more likely to accept your suggested price when they see concrete facts rather than some figure they think you arbitrarily pulled out of your hat.

So, with the Comparative Market Analysis, not only are you selling yourself and impressing potential sellers with your professionalism and thoroughness, you are paving the way for a listing that is priced to sell!

BUILDING YOUR COMPARATIVE MARKET ANALYSIS

Present your Comparative Market Analysis in much the same form as you present your marketing presentation, but as a separate and distinct report. Be sure you do a cover page for your Comparative Market Analysis so you can provide a distinctive break between the marketing and pricing parts of your listing presentation. Remember, I suggest putting all of the materials in a company folder or some other professional-looking folder for your presentation.

Start the analysis with another cover page that says:

My Comparative Market Analysis for
(Seller's name)

Prepared and Presented by
(Your name, title, and company)

Below are listed the sheets of information and facts I suggest you place in your Comparative Market Analysis of your Detailed Report. Place them right after your cover page mentioned earlier.

Estimate of Seller's Net Proceeds

Most companies have their own form for this, so I suggest using your company's form. Leave this form blank in this part of the report. I normally don't fill this one in for them because I am not ready for them to see the suggested list price yet. I don't want to tell them my suggested price in the first part of the meeting. You don't want the sellers to be distracted from looking at the comparables you have brought with you by hearing the price at this point. Who has control of this presentation? You do. So wait until the very end to get into the actual suggested price.

Do put the form in here so you won't forget to have it available when someone makes an offer on the house. By putting a blank form here, you can simply say, "Now, Sally and John, this is the form we will fill out at a later time based on an estimate of a sale price. I've kept a blank one in your file so that at the time of the purchase and sale agreement I'll know we have one right here." Then you can tell them, "We will do an estimate of your proceeds at the end of the presentation today, and look at the figures at that time."

Multiple Listing Service Statistics

I believe the multiple's statistics are very important. Sellers need to see the average selling price of homes in your area, so they can understand the market, at large, in a better way. Not all your sellers' homes will fit the statistics you will find, but remember, these are averages. Explain to them that is why you are showing the statistics to them.

Take statistics from the front of your MLS book, if they are available to you, or use the statistics from the computer. If they are not in your book or computer, talk to your multiple listing association and find out how you can get the statistics showing what is going on in your area, either weekly, monthly, or even yearly. These statistics tell you the total number of properties for sale in your particular area. Let's say your area is averaging over 11,000 total properties in your whole multiple, including single-family homes, condominium homes, land, and individual lots. Break those figures down and point out to your sellers that in total volume, there are, for instance, 5,739 single-family homes for sale in your area. You could say, "So, you can see, that's a lot of competition." You are already educating your potential sellers on the current market.

Changing Times

When I started selling real estate years ago, we had less than one thousand homes for sale in my area. The typical purchaser might look at three homes and purchase one of them. You might have had a similar experience in real estate, so share that bit of history with your sellers in order to build your case for the price you have set on their property. You can say, "But what we see today is the complete opposite of that. Because in a slower market when we have so many properties listed, most purchasers want to look at a lot of homes. I have agents telling me some clients look at fifty, seventy-five, even more than one hundred homes before they make a decision." Tell them about that condition, if it is true for your area, so they realize competition is very strong. You may be in an active selling area, so share how that is affecting the way purchasers view and buy homes. So, whatever the market, educate your sellers with the real facts of what is going on in their area.

Show them statistics for their category of home or condominium and highlight not only the average list price and average selling price, but the average market time as well. Spend plenty of time on this and bring up any statistics you think are pertinent for your area. You want them to have a firm grip of what your market is doing. I cannot stress this point with you too much!

Ask for Commitments. Let's say that the average time on the market for the typical three-bedroom in your area might be 111 days. The average time on the market for the sale of a four-bedroom home could be 125 days. Now is a good time to ask for a commitment from your sellers on the length of time you will list their property. When I come to this part of the analysis, I lean over, and right in front of them, I write with my pen on the statistics sheet "three to six months." You would write whatever the average length of selling time is in your market. I write it out in big letters, and I underline it. I do this and point out to them the following: "Now, Sally and John, as you have just seen in part one of my report, I have made a lot of marketing commitments to you. These are serious commitments that work. I am proud of these commitments. But, just as in any relationship, there should be commitments on both sides. So, I also ask commitments of both of you as well. I ask just two commitments. The first one is that, with your permission, you will allow me to go through your home room by room to make suggestions to prepare it for sale." What I've done here is to ask them for an easy commitment; one that doesn't come as a surprise because we've already discussed it. But I ask them anyway.

Note that I like to start all my requests with "With your permission..." People like to cooperate. They don't like to take orders.

Then I continue by saying, "And the second commitment I ask, Sally and John, is a six-month listing period in which to get the job done. Now, I would like to share a couple of things with you, Sally and John. I'm the last one who wants it to take six months to get your home sold. But, as you can see, the average sale is taking place between the third and the sixth month (this is another reason I showed them the statistics). So, as a businesswoman (or businessman), it just doesn't make sense for me to list properties for less than six months when the average sale is not taking place until between the third and sixth month." I continue to tell them that for as long as we have had this kind of market, I have not listed a property for less than six months.

You must adapt this to your own circumstances and market selling time. Now, if you've done this correctly, you showed the sellers the average selling time. They know the enormous commitment you have just made to them in your marketing program. They know what each commitment is because you've shown it to them in writing and you've gone over it in detail by showing it in your *Marketing Portfolio.* So, by now, they know you are going to be doing a lot of work. Because you have educated them so well, most sellers aren't bothered in the least to list for a period of six months or whatever time frame you specify.

If the properties in your area are selling in a matter of two to four weeks, you don't need to use the three- to six-month figure. Just fill in the blanks with the figures that apply to your area.

You are developing a relationship— a partnership. It would not be fair for you to make serious, dedicated commitments while the other people in that partnership don't make any. I usually have no problem at all getting sellers to make those two commitments by doing it the way I have just described to you.

Comparables

After I've gone over my statistics, I want to acquaint my sellers with the actual competition. In this section, I have listing prices and facts about homes similar to my sellers' property. I want them to see exactly what properties are out there and what prices they are bringing. This information can add more impact to the statistics they have just seen. I suggest you show your sellers comparables from the following areas: solds, expireds, current competition on the market, and properties that have been taken off the market. I might say something like: "Sally and John, these are the comparables I have brought for you to see. It is important for you to see these properties because it is the best way for us to see how we fit into the market together."

Which areas do I check for comparables? I usually take the whole section of the book where my sellers' property is located. If you can break it down by smaller neighborhoods in your area, that's great, but I find that most of today's purchasers look at many different neighborhoods before they ever settle on one, and the sellers need to be told that. I don't include other sections of the book that aren't pertinent to my sellers' property; however,

I will tell my sellers that potential purchasers can also be looking in those other areas as well.

I like to bring several types of comparables for my sellers to see. Almost all of us now have computers available to us, and that's terrific. One thing I have observed, however, is that when I have only used computer printouts with my sellers, they have had a hard time relating to them. For example, I would lay out this long computer printout— about six pages hooked all together— with all the facts and figures. They would look at it, but they had no way to really form mental pictures of the homes. So, I bring it all: pictures, printouts, and multiple listings. If your multiple still uses a book that has pictures, I suggest you use it. Sellers just seem to relate to it better than cold computer statistics. I go back through the multiple books and highlight the figures and statistics about houses that were on the market, what they sold for, the length of time it took them to sell, and the terms under which they were sold. I do bring computer printouts, and I lay them out with the homes I've taken from the multiple book and circled. I suggest you use both— actually anything you can get. It is really strong ammunition for showing your sellers what is going on in their area. That way, you can highlight the appropriate factors, then go over all of them with your sellers, home by home.

Visit Your Comparables. I try to visit as many of the comparables as I can. That way I can talk about them with much more knowledge. Obviously I don't have enough time to see them all. So, I try to see the two or three properties closest to the home for which I am doing the analysis— at least those I think are the best buys that have sold (but not closed) in the last two to three months. If you have a lot of sales, of course, it's a good idea to check houses that have been sold in the last month, week, or day or two. Be sure you check out the homes in the sellers' immediate neighborhood. You'd be surprised how knowledge-able some people are about their neighbors, and you don't want to be embarrassed if they know more than you do.

Getting the Most Impact. Here is how I go over the comparables with my sellers: "This home sold $10,000 below what they were asking for it, and here is why.... This home took almost a year to sell, and this is my professional opinion of why I think it took so long...."

I go over each one of them, giving them my opinions of why they did or didn't sell. By using this technique, you can build credibility for the price you have determined is most appropriate for their home. It also helps to include a home that has a floor plan that is a little different from theirs but has some of the same amenities. If they have a hot tub and swimming pool, you should find comparable houses that have those features.

After I have gone over all the homes that have sold, I do the very same thing for all those currently on the market. I might say something like, "Sally and John, now we need to see what we are going to be competing with when we come on the market together. I want you to see what is really out there." I point out to them how long each house has been on the market. Has it been on the market for six months? Why? Is it getting what we call "shop worn?" I explain to them how you can get "shop worn" if you are on the market too long. I point out such things as terms. Do these houses offer good terms? Are they open to FHA or VA financing? What about a deed of trust? I also go over the size of the lots and the actual square footage of the property. We discuss everything in comparison to the sellers' home.

I also believe in showing sellers a few appropriate expired listings in the same way that I showed solds and active listings. This is your opportunity to drive home some important points as to why these particular properties didn't sell. Usually it is very easy to pinpoint things such as location, staging, condition, and particularly price. (If you research expired listings in almost any category you will usually find that the average price of all expired listings is ten to fifteen percent higher than the average price of sold homes.)

STAGED HOMES

This concept is very important! With all of the comparables I show the sellers, including solds, on-the-market competition, or expired listings, I always point out to the sellers if the comparable property was *Staged* or not. I'll say, for example, "This home sold full price in one week, and it had been *Staged.*" Then I reinforce that with the fact that *Staged* homes always sell faster and/or for more money. Of course, I point out the homes that did not sell were usually not *Staged,* were overpriced, or both.

This then constantly keeps emphasizing how truly important *Staging* the sellers' home is. Try it, it works.

LAYING THE GROUNDWORK

It is very important that you take the time to present your Comparative Market Analysis so your sellers can have a thorough understanding of the market and the competition. If you take plenty of time and cover all the areas that I have shared with you in this chapter, you will find your sellers will be more cooperative and understanding when it's time to price their home, which is the next step in your listing presentation.

11

Recipe for a Sale: Pricing the Property Right

In this chapter you will learn

1. What are the ingredients of a sale.
2. How the ingredients of a sale can help sellers understand pricing for their home.
3. How to fill out and use a pricing triangle to help you establish list price with your sellers.

A Comparative Market Analysis explains to your sellers what is happening in their market. Next, you want to show your sellers the price you have determined that is appropriate for their home and what facts you used to make that determination.

SETTING THE LIST PRICE: INGREDIENTS OF A SALE

One of my best sayings follows:

> **Just like the product on the shelf at the store, the purchaser of today buys the best available product, for the best price, in the best package, to meet his or her needs.**

Throughout your Comparative Market Analysis, you have shown your sellers what is happening in the market and what price comparable properties in their area are bringing. Now you can talk about the price you feel is most suitable for the sellers' property, and how you arrived at this figure. Again, you don't want to throw a figure at them without first giving them some facts. Therefore, before we look at the "Pricing Your Home" triangle, I always go through what I call the "ingredients of a sale."

I know that five main ingredients must work together before you can sell a home. I used to sit down with sellers and talk all about the elements of a sale. After a while I started to refer to it as a "Recipe For a Sale." I found out quickly, my sellers could relate better to this than to a sea of figures.

So, before you reveal the price you have estimated for your sellers' home, go over each of the ingredients of a sale. When you educate your sellers on the importance of each of these five ingredients, you won't be burdened with overpriced listings that are in terrible condition.

Ingredient 1: Location

I borrow a favorite phrase of appraisers to explain to my sellers how important location is in the sale of a home: "You have to consider three things when figuring the price of a home: location, location, and location."

Explain to your sellers that some homes are simply in better locations than others, and the location of a home will be reflected in its price. Talk to sellers in direct relation to their home's location. For example, if a home is on a great spot on a cul-de-sac where there isn't a lot of traffic, point that out as a plus to the sellers. If it is on a busy street, don't let your sellers shut their eyes to that fact. It is your job to be honest with your sellers, and to tell them when you feel their location may be working against them. It is your job to help the sellers price their property right, and you can't do that if you don't help them look at it objectively. Remember, you are the expert, and you have done the work to arrive at the suggested list price. Doctors, lawyers, and accountants all stick to their professional opinions because they are the professionals. You and I must do the same when it comes to our profession. It is in the best interest of our sellers and ourselves.

Ingredient 2: Condition

The upkeep and presentation of a property is crucial to obtain the highest value for it. You cannot stress this enough when talking with your sellers. This is true in any given market at any given time. Sometimes the things you and I see as agents are just unbelievable. Some people do not take care of their homes during the years they live there. For example, they have been there ten years, the roof is leaking, the carpets are worn, the house needs painting, and all of a sudden they want to bring it on the market. They have some catching up to do. If they are unwilling to improve the condition of that property, the price is going to reflect it. If you come across sellers who fit this description, point out to them how important condition is. They will have to fix up the home or settle for a lower price.

I believe that *Staging*, which I will discuss at length in a later chapter, is different from *condition*. If the roof leaks, you have to price it accordingly and, of course, disclose it. If the furnace is broken, you have to price it accordingly and, of course, disclose it. *Staging*, conversely, has to do with how the property *shows* according to clutter, clean, and color. *Staging* can influence price, especially in an active market. In most markets

Staging helps most with the length of selling time. No matter what the market is doing, I always *Stage* the house as it pays off every time in every market. So, I always price a home knowing I can get it *Staged.*

Ingredient 3: Price

If an old friend said to me, "Barb, tell me the truth. What is the number one thing that gets property sold?" I would have to say the price. Pricing is the number one factor in the sale of any home. You and I know that, and it is our job to help our sellers understand it.

A property is only worth what one person is willing to pay another to gain ownership of it. Price must reflect the other four ingredients. I really stress with sellers that pricing is the most important and influential ingredient. You can take any property, anywhere, in any condition, and eventually it will sell— if it has the right market price on it. This is a good place in your presentation to share this with your sellers.

Here, also, is a good place to explain to sellers that the appraised value of a home and its selling price can be two different things. Sometimes you come across a couple who has never marketed a house, and who has already hired a fee appraiser to come in and determine what the house is worth. Then all of a sudden, you come in with your Comparative Market Analysis and a completely different price. Say, "Remember, Mr. and Mrs. Seller, a home is only worth what one individual is willing to pay for it. We do not know at this time what that will actually be because you have not sold yet; we are just coming on the market." When you are working in a buyer's market it is especially crucial for your sellers to understand this point.

Ingredient 4: Terms

The more attractive the terms available on a property, the more potential purchasers you can reach. The seller who is able to offer FHA and VA loans, or a deed of trust, in addition to conventional financing, leaves the door wide open for many more potential purchasers. Every additional term opens the door a little wider. Remind your future sellers that the opposite is also true.

Ingredient 5: The Market

Now when I say "the market," I am talking about several things, including interest rates, competition, and the economy. All of these factors influence the state of the market when you sell your home. And, once again, the price of a home must reflect the current status of the market. If there is one thing we cannot control, it is the market. Take plenty of time to discuss the market you are in right now in your area. No matter whether it is hot or not, it is really worth the time it takes to educate your future sellers. Do it now, because it will really pay off down the road as you work with them.

Combine Ingredients; Stir Well. When all of the preceding ingredients are in harmony, you have a sale. If just one of them is out of line, it will take longer to sell the property. The more the ingredients are out of line, the longer it will probably take. Make sure your sellers understand this. For example, let's say the home is in a good location, but its condition is questionable. Because those two ingredients are not quite in balance, the sellers will have to settle for a lower price, possibly wait a long time before they sell, or bring the condition up to where it should be.

You must explain to your future sellers how important it is to have all of the ingredients in balance. You cannot usually move a house and you cannot change the market, but most sellers, when it really comes down to it, can balance price, terms, and condition. They have to realize this, or they will simply sit there and not sell.

PRICING TRIANGLE

It is your job to tell your sellers where you feel they fit in today's market in price and terms. So, the last page in your presentation packet should be the "Pricing Your Home" triangle (Figure 11-1). Fill it out ahead of time! Don't meet with your sellers for your listing presentation without a written statement on the price you believe is suitable for their home. But, to control the flow and timing of your presentation, it is important to leave this to the very end.

Pricing Your Home

There are ___57___ homes for sale in your area

priced between $180,000.00 and $195,000.00

The total number of homes on the market is ___4,210___

We Cannot Control:
Location
The Market, i.e.
  Interest Rates
  Competition
  Economy

We Can Control:
Condition
Price
Terms

$ ___195,000.00___ up ↑

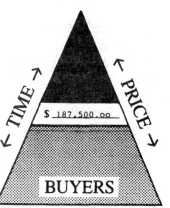

$ ___187,500.00___

$ ___180,000.00___ down ↓

Homes For Sale On The Market

FIGURE 11–1   "Pricing Your Home" Triangle

After you finish reviewing the "Recipe For a Sale" with your sellers, turn to the page with the pricing triangle and the price you recommend for their home. Tell your sellers, "As I turn the page, I have a pricing triangle with the pricing for your home."

Always point out that the facts and figures on the pricing triangle came right from the comparable homes you just looked at together in the Comparative Market Analysis.

How to Use the Pricing Triangle

As you can see on the sample diagram, at the top of the page you can include some information on the number of comparable homes in the sellers' area. For example, you might point to the top of the page and say to the sellers, "I've counted all the homes in your area that fit in this price range. There are fifty-seven homes for sale in your area priced between $180,000 and $195,000. That is a lot of competition!"

Do count all of the homes in their area for sale. Why? You and I both know how many times a buyer will say to us, "Only show me one-level homes." And they end up buying a two-story house. I rest my case. Count all of the homes for sale in their area as competition!

CONTROLLABLE VERSUS UNCONTROLLABLE INGREDIENTS

To explain these elements, I recommend that you say the following: "In addition to these figures, Mr. and Mrs. Seller, I have divided the list of ingredients for a sale into two categories—ingredients you cannot control and those you can. As a seller of a resale home you cannot control the location of a property. You cannot control the market, which includes interest rates, the competition, and the economy. It would be nice if you could keep the prime rate at 8 percent. But you cannot control the market. You are at the mercy of such variables. But you can usually control three very important ingredients— condition, price, and terms."

Most sellers can control the condition of their property, or at least they can do something about it. And even though sometimes sellers don't want to admit it, they can control the price of their property. You see this in properties that have been on the market for a long time. Some of them have dropped their asking price $50,000 to $100,000 in order to sell. Others in a lower price range have dropped $5,000 or $10,000. They had to drop because they started out significantly overpriced. Even though they felt when they started that they couldn't control the price, they *had* to control the price in the end to sell the property. Explain all this to your sellers. They need to understand the impact that price has on the sale of their home.

Many people don't consider terms a controllable ingredient. Sellers will sometimes say, "Well, I really can't take any paper. I've got to be totally cashed out of the property." But after they have been on the market for a while, all of a sudden they will agree to hold $5,000 in the form of a deed of trust for that purchaser. So, you see, terms can be controllable. Use this example to explain that to your sellers.

THE RIGHT PRICE

I suggest that you write three prices on the triangle before you meet with each seller for your listing presentation—the highest price you would list the home at, the lowest price you would list it at, and the price you would really like to list it for optimum price and selling time. For example, let's say at the bottom you have written $180,000. Beside that bottom figure it says "down" with a little arrow pointing downward beside it. That, of course, means exactly that—$180,000 and lower. The $180,000 is the lowest price at which you think the property should be priced. And that is the figure you fill in at the bottom of the triangle. Yes, there is a lowest price! Recent court cases have decided in favor of sellers who have sued their real estate broker for lost dollars because their home was listed and sold for too little.

In the middle of the triangle, write the price you are recommending for the property—let's say, $187,500. At the top of the triangle, insert the high price, which, for this example, is $195,000. Beside that figure it says "up" with a little arrow pointing upward. The $195,000, is the highest price at which you will take the listing and still expect to sell it. You have a responsibility to yourself and a legal responsibility to your sellers not to price the property too high.

Here's how I would explain the pricing triangle to sellers: "Sally and John, here is a triangle. I call it the 'Pricing Your Home' triangle. I find that it really helps sellers understand the pricing of their home. At the very bottom I have written in

$180,000. Now, I want to set your mind to rest that I am not suggesting we list your home at $180,000. But you see, at the bottom of the triangle, we have a very wide base, which means we would have a lot of 'buyers' at that price. The lower we price your property, the more potential purchasers there will be and the faster your home will sell. As we move up in price on the triangle several things take place. I've written the words 'price' and 'time' on either side of the triangle to show that as the price goes up, so does the length of time it takes to sell a home. In other words, the higher we move in pricing, the longer it will take to sell your home. Notice that because buyers are on the inside of the triangle the higher we go in price, the fewer number of buyers there are for your home. I've shaded in the upper section of the triangle to demonstrate that the higher the price climbs, the tougher it gets to sell the home. At $195,000 you can see that it would be difficult to sell your home because there would be very few buyers at the top of the pricing triangle.

"The price I recommend we come on the market with is $187,500, which is the price in the middle. This is a fair market price where your property should sell in a reasonable period."

Notice that not only does the triangle demonstrate how price and time are related, it makes it even clearer by showing them how they work together. This really does help sellers understand the importance of pricing their home right.

BOTTOM LINE

The idea I am about to share with you has enabled me to help a lot of sellers price their property right. After you have gone over the triangle, move to the line drawn across the bottom of the page that is right above "Homes For Sale On The Market." This line represents homes for sale on the market today, and you can use it to get sellers to look objectively at the pricing of their home. You can use this approach with your sellers just the way I am relating it to you.

I draw a line to represent the market. Then I divide it into thirds, which represents almost exactly the three states of our market. Statistics from all over the nation have proved this, except in the most active markets. Even in those markets, however, most of this idea is true. Again, I do this right there in front of the sellers.

Let's talk about a home that fits into the first third on the right. This home is a "never sell." It could be a mess, or on a busy street. The condition may be horrible. The roof leaks. The carpet is worn, or it needs painting. It is overpriced or in a bad location. As I tell my sellers about this house, I lean over in front of them, and I scrawl the word "NEVER" on that first third. I write it in big letters, and I underline it. This third will never sell— unless the owners change one or more ingredients of the sale. They would have to drop the price, or they could change the condition. But as long as things stay the way they are— overpriced, poor location, or bad condition— it will never sell. Houses like this can sit on the market for years, and they are out there today in every market.

In the middle third of the line, I lean over in front of the sellers and scribble a big question mark. This house could go either way. Somebody might buy it, but the word is might. There are no buyers standing in line to purchase this home. The location is not too bad, but the corner is way too busy. The condition is not horrible; however, the place is priced higher than most of the others. Buyers usually won't leave this property on their list. It's just a question mark. The buyers looking through these kinds of properties usually say, "Well, this seller will have to get lucky, but not with my money. I am not buying it."

How many sellers have you heard say, "Let's just try it at this price, maybe we'll get lucky"? Sharing this truth about what buyers think and say when looking at homes priced in this third before the sellers get to talking about "lucky," really heads the objection off up front. So, I explain to my sellers this third of the market is a real question mark.

We have to do our job and share our professional opinions with sellers. Look them right in the eyes and say, "There is no 'getting lucky' in real estate. We cannot just see what happens or just try to get lucky. When sellers do try this they usually end up losing even more later on by having to lower their price even further to get the buyers back in their front door."

The National Association of Realtors® statistics support this idea and you can show these figures to your sellers if you like (Figure 11-2). The chart simply shows that the longer a home is on the market, the lower the selling price of that property will

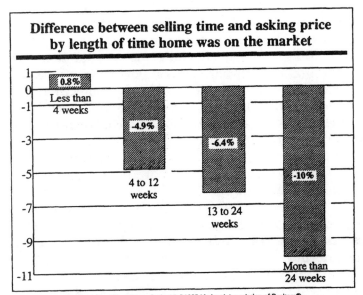

Reprinted from "Real Estate Outlook" ©1987 National Association of Realtors®

FIGURE 11-2 Difference between Selling Time and Asking Price

be. These statistics prove that pricing the property right in the beginning will bring your sellers a quicker, more profitable sale.

Then we have the final third. I lean over and say, "This is the third of the market that is hot. This is the third of the market that sells." I write, in big letters, the word "YES!" on that third. This is the third that buyers go into and say, "This is exciting! This home looks better than the other two-thirds we just looked at, and it is priced equal to or lower than the other two-thirds." Tell your sellers that this is where they need to be! To have a sale in the quickest, fairest amount of time, the property needs to be priced right, look great, and be in a good location. The better your sellers understand this, the easier it is for you to price the property right. This final third is where you want all your listings to be. In this third of the market, all the ingredients of the sale work together.

Using a line to divide the market into thirds is a great idea! You can talk about the ingredients of the sale as well as the length of selling time. From the "YES!" third all the way over to the "NEVER" third, you have just moved from selling in a short amount of time to probably never selling. You can also adapt prices to the line, simply moving them from the triangle to the appropriate third you have just drawn. As you move the prices to the line, you could say, "If we set the price for your house at $220,000, we are going to fit the "never sell" third. If we are selling at $195,000, frankly, it is still a question mark. We just don't know. However, at $180,000 to $187,500, we are going to fit the "YES!" third— the hot category!" So, write in prices there, too, if you like.

REFUSAL OF A LISTING

People occasionally ask me, "Do you take overpriced listings?" I admit it! I have taken overpriced listings. We all end up doing it at one time or another. The key is to not take listings that are way overpriced and totally out of sight. If I meet sellers whose motivations I feel will change, then I go ahead and list it at the *top* of the price range, as long as they fit *into* the price range on the triangle. I have already given myself some leeway in the pricing triangle. But if the sellers want to go *above* the highest price on my triangle, then I will let the listing go. Once I have done my Comparative Market Analysis and determined the prices on my "Pricing Your Home" triangle, this is where I professionally think the property should be listed. If the sellers want to come on higher or lower than that, I will not take the listing. Having professional policies and being honest wins, I find, in the long run.

Ways to Turn Down Sellers

Now, this brings us to an interesting question. How do you turn down sellers? For example, let's say you have sellers who you would really like to work with. You love the house, and you'd really like to list it, but the sellers are not yet motivated to sell. How do you turn down the listing, but still leave the door open so they will want you to list the house later?

The commitments you have made to the sellers in the marketing portion of your Detailed Report leave you a perfect solution. So, when you think you shouldn't take a listing, look at your sellers and say, "Sally and John, I just love your home. I really do. And I would very much like to represent you as your exclusive listing agent. But, at this time, I cannot enthusiastically support listing the property at that price, with all my marketing techniques and efforts."

Now, you see, by saying "at this time" leaves the door open for the future. And "I cannot enthusiastically support" lets you off the hook. No one would want you to list his or her property if you weren't enthusiastic about it. It is a perfect way of saying to your sellers, "Later on you may be ready to sell— and I hope you are— and I'll be there at that time to bring your home on the market with you. At that time, I will enthusiastically support it with everything that I've got." With all the commitments you have made to them, they understand you need that enthusiasm. Then add, "Down the road, chances are that you are going to need me. And I am going to be right here ready to go to work for you. I will really look forward to that time. And I want to keep in touch. I would like for you to call if you have any questions at all. If you decide not to go on the market, and you want to look at my Exclusive Marketing Program and Comparative Market Analysis again, let's sit down and review it. But the important thing I want you to know is that I have enjoyed meeting you, I love your home, and I am ready to go to work for you as soon as we can enthusiastically come on the market together at a competitive price."

You have left the door wide open! I know this works. I have had sellers call me later and say, "OK, Barb, we're ready to go. Get yourself over here and list our home." "Terrific!" I say. "Is three o'clock good, or is four o'clock better?" (Hint: Never tell them, "I told you so" about pricing.) When your sellers call you back, meet with them again and be prepared to present a new market analysis, because prices may have changed. If the figures haven't changed, take the opportunity to re-educate them. Review your marketing and pricing with them all over again, because sometimes a lot has happened in their lives and some time has passed. Educating your sellers, even if you have to go over something twice, is not a waste of time!

LISTING AGREEMENT

The last point to cover in your presentation is the listing agreement. Always carry a blank form in your packet when you make a presentation. For those sellers who are ready to list, fill it out with them blank by blank. Of course you want to fill it out right then. Once in a great while, after you have given your presentation, you and your sellers do not have the time to complete the paper work right then; however, be sure to get the sellers' verbal commitment before you leave. Set the time to return to fill out the paper work together and *Stage* the house. Once your sellers decide to hire you as their listing agent, don't worry that they will change their minds if you have to come back for step three and fill out the listing. The key is to ask for their business. Tell the sellers you really do want to be their agent, and you are ready to go to work for them. The sellers should be so excited about how you are going to market their home that they would not even consider going on the market with anyone else— especially once they have said to you, "We're ready to go! We want you to list our home." When they ask, "Where do we sign?" you know you have done it all the right way. It is the ultimate when you don't even have to ask the sellers for their business. You'll soon see this reaction from your sellers when you start using all the techniques, ideas, tools, and tips I am presenting in this book!

12

Step 3:
Listing the Property

In this chapter you will learn

1. Details to watch for in the listing agreement.
2. How to capture some interesting facts about your sellers' property.
3. The importance of getting a seller's signature before you begin to *Stage* their home and begin your service.

As the listing agent, it is your job to guide your sellers through the process of listing their home. Because you have educated them throughout your first two visits (steps) about the importance of preparing their property for sale, your sellers, if they are motivated, will welcome your professional opinion. Once the sellers authorize you to list their property, the real work—and the fun—begins. The listing agreement must be filled out correctly, and the house must be prepared for the market. If you want to represent your sellers' properties accurately, you must complete the listing accurately.

Now for the part you have been waiting for—completing the listing agreement with the sellers! Remember two rules when you come to this part of the game: Be careful and be complete.

CAREFUL APPROACH

Many of us love to have our listing agreements typed out ahead of time. It looks so professional and can help everyone involved. But I want to caution you about mistakes. If it is completely typed ahead of time, especially if someone else types it, an error might slip past you. I recommend you have only three blanks filled out in advance—the name of your company, the date the agreement expires, and the fee you are charging.

You are responsible for the listing agreement, so be very careful to check every line with your sellers, even if it is typed ahead of time. You cannot be too cautious! Take the time to go over *every* blank with your sellers. Ask your sellers every single question on the listing agreement. You may have put down four bedrooms, and you forgot about the room in the basement that could qualify as a fifth bedroom. Ask them the questions with even apparently obvious answers.

ATTENTION TO DETAILS

Although I strongly suggest you go over every line of the agreement, it is a good idea to pay extra special attention to certain areas.

Numbers, Numbers, Numbers

Be sure all your figures are correct. This includes lot size, room dimensions in certain areas of the country, and square footage. It is crucial that you represent the property accurately. Always make certain you have the correct legal description of the property and the proper address. As far as property taxes are concerned, find out the taxes for the year in which you are actually listing the property.

Key Boxes

As discussed earlier, I think these are vital. Now, I realize this varies from area to area and region to region. But, if key boxes (called lock boxes or key safes in some areas) are traditional in your particular area, make certain your sellers understand why it is so important to have this means of access to the property. If people can't get in, how can they see the house and property?

General Remarks

Get remarks from your sellers about their home that will help you describe their property. Ask them to describe all the things about their home they really enjoy— the location, the large deck or family room, any nearby conveniences, the schools, the parks— all the facts which would interest a potential purchaser. You can discover some dynamite selling points that way! Take out a big sheet of paper and start writing as fast as you can. Let them talk and talk, as long as they want. You may come up with some great adjectives you can use when it comes time for you to write an information sheet, a flyer, or ads.

REVIEW LISTING AGREEMENT

After you have reviewed the entire listing agreement together, then it is time for the sellers to check what you have written and then give you their authorization. Hand them the agreement, and say, "Mr. and Mrs. Seller, would you please review this entire listing agreement now before you authorize it?"

Take the time now to be sure they look it over. I never like to see the sellers just grab hold of the paper and then sign at the bottom without looking it over. I want them to know what they are signing. This is part of the education process. Yes, it takes a little longer, because you are going to be sitting there while they are reviewing it. But this prevents future problems. If they read the agreement they are signing, chances are they will catch errors and any possible misunderstandings now. That can save you time and headaches later. So sit, wait, and watch. Offer to answer any questions they might have. Make sure they read the small print on the agreement, too. Only after they have reviewed the agreement should they be ready to give their authorization.

SELLERS' LISTING PACKET

After the sellers have authorized the listing agreement, give them a copy of everything. Give them their own listing packet, just as you said you would when you made your listing presentation. You should also tear off a copy of the listing agreement and include it too.

Ask your sellers to keep their packet in a special place, preferably out of sight. Tell them, "It's personal, it's yours, and it's private. So, let's not leave it out on the kitchen table." If you agree on where they are going to keep their packet, then you have a private place where you can leave the sellers notes from time to time. For example, when they return after a brokers' or a public open house, they know they can go to the drawer where they keep their listing folder packet and find a note from you about the open house. Why not just leave notes on the dining room table or the kitchen table? Again, purchasers and other agents are coming through that property, and your sellers deserve privacy. You might want to leave a note to remind your sellers of some things they still need to do, such as turn on the lights for the showings. You wouldn't want an agent or purchaser reading those notes.

The work doesn't stop after you and your sellers have completed the listing agreement. It really has just begun. But you have been waiting for this moment. The sooner you can get those information sheets prepared and back on the sellers' dining room table, the better. That way, as soon as the house is ready to show, your information center for purchasers and other agents will be ready.

Now on to the fun part— *Staging* the sellers home with them. But remember:

> **Get the sellers' signatures before you give your service of *Staging* their home.**

If you were to *Stage* the sellers' property with them before they signed the listing agreement, you would put yourself in a vulnerable position. Reversing the order just isn't a good idea. I learned that from an experience I had when I *Staged* a home before I had the owners' commitment in writing. I hope it will save you from the same mistake.

Do you remember this story at the beginning of the book? Remember, early in my career, I eagerly helped a For Sale by Owner *Stage* her own property for sale, on my first visit to her home. I was trying to impress her and her husband. I made recommendations in every room. I helped her move some furniture, rehang some pictures, put things away in the kitchen, and so forth. We covered about everything. Then, because it was getting late and they were having dinner guests, she asked me to give my listing presentation the next day. When I returned the next day to do just that, they told me they had sold the house the night before— to their dinner guests. The sellers said to me, "When we sat down to eat, our friends said the house had never looked so good. They were so impressed with what they saw, they bought it!"

I made the crucial error of giving those potential sellers all my expertise before they gave me their written commitment. You can give tips to the sellers so they know you know what you are doing, but don't do the actual *Staging* with them until they have signed on the bottom line. Offering a lot of suggestions for improving a property for sale is a valuable service, so be sure you have the listing signed before you start giving advice. Otherwise, some other agent might profit from your ideas, or the For Sale by Owner could sell his or her own home, as in the case I just described.

After you have gone through everything on the listing agreement, the sellers have signed it, and they have their packet and a copy of the agreement, then you can begin to *Stage* their home!

13

Staging™ *the Property: The Inside Story*

In this chapter you will learn

1. The importance of telling your sellers what needs to be done to prepare their house for sale.
2. How to tell your sellers what needs to be done to prepare their home for sale.
3. The three C's of *Staging*.
4. My "Tips for Selling," which you can share with your sellers for the inside of their home.

The way a home shows is one of the few ingredients for a sale that you can help control. To get the best price for a property, it needs to be in top-notch showing condition. The best part is that it's really easy to do. Let me tell you how.

CONQUEST OF FEAR

This really is the fun part! I love to *Stage* homes. And when you teach your sellers, up front, that this will help them get the most amount of equity in the shortest amount of time, they will love to *Stage* their home with you, too. The following is one of my best sayings, and one of the most important concepts you should teach your sellers:

> **The way we live in a home and the way we sell a home are two different things.**

I have worked with a lot of agents in my seminars and programs, and I have yet to find one who isn't interested in helping sellers get their property ready to sell. After all, the better the home shows, the faster the sale, and/or the higher the selling price, which means more commission! Many times, though, we just don't know quite what to tell sellers, or we are afraid to tell them what we do know.

For the first few months I was in this business I was afraid to tell my sellers what to do to prepare their homes to sell. I knew what to tell my sellers, but I was afraid I would upset them or hurt their feelings. And here I was, a former interior designer! I learned, however, we can say almost anything to our sellers. Sellers have even said, "It's OK. Just tell us what to do. You're not going to hurt our feelings." You can be sure your motivated sellers want to know what they can do to get a better price for their home! And that is the key: motivation. Sellers who are motivated want to know because they want their equity, or money, out of their home. It will be difficult to convince sellers who are not really motivated to move that they need to *Stage* their home.

I have worked with agents who have said to me, "Barb, I am really afraid to tell my sellers what to do." One gentleman, who was sixty-five years old, said, "I've been in another line of work all my life, and now I'm just starting to sell real estate. I don't even know what to tell them to do." I put into his hands some of the same tools I am going to give you in the next few chapters, and he has been a believer ever since! By the time he got to *Staging* the house, he told me, "I don't believe it. These people are eating out of my hand. They love what I do. They've taken every suggestion. They've even said, 'Tell us more! Tell us more!' I can't believe the power I've had. It has been incredible!" You can feel incredible, too!

Remember, *Staging* is not new to sellers. You have talked about *Staging* from the very first time you met. They heard you tell them about *Staging* when you said, "Let me tell you how I work." They saw it twice in your *Career Book*. You went over it in detail during the marketing section of your Detailed Report in the listing presentation. You even showed them pictures of other homes you have *Staged*. And it was at that time that you asked them for their commitment to let you *Stage* their home with them. This is not new news at this point in the process! Sellers want you to *Stage* their home, and if you have educated them all along, they will expect it.

It is time in our industry that we stop thinking sellers don't want us to help them *Stage* their properties. We have been the only industry I can think of to bring the merchandise on the market for sale "as is" just because we were afraid of hurting our clients' feelings. Remember, doctors, attorneys, accountants, and other professionals are going to tell their clients the truth because they owe them that. And, so do we! If you don't tell them, then who will? Plus, if you approach *Staging* the property in the right way, you and your sellers are going to have a lot of fun doing it together.

I'm going to prove to you right now that sellers really do want us to *Stage* their homes. Remember the For Sale by Owner I've talked about twice in this book? The one who said, "yes" when I asked if they would want to know ideas that would help them sell their home? They almost begged me for it. Well, here is something I want to ask you: If the For Sale by Owners would want to know anything and everything that could help them sell their home, including *Staging*, and get the information for free, then why would a regular seller who is listing with you and paying you thousands and thousands of dollars in commissions *not* want to know? Just asking myself this question changed my career forever! I am convinced that agents must *Stage* homes. Sellers need it and want it. It is your responsibility to help them.

GREAT IDEA: THE CAR STORY

If you run into sellers who do not seem to understand the concept of *Staging*, ask them one simple question, "If you were going to sell your car, what would you do to it before you showed it to any potential purchasers?" Wait for their answer. They will invariably tell you: "I'd wash it, wax it, vacuum it, clean out the junk, and touch up the chips." They may even talk about fixing other problems. Agree with your sellers, "That's what I would do, too."

Then ask your sellers where most people's money or equity is: "In our homes or in our cars?" Wait for the answer, which invariably is, "in our homes." Then add, "Well, do you know that many sellers on the market today have not done with their own homes what they have done with their cars to bring them on the market for sale? They haven't gotten them ready to sell. By preparing your home for sale, we will be much further ahead of most of our competition." The car story works because it really gets your sellers thinking about where their money is and about what they should do to prepare their homes for sale.

THREE C'S OF STAGING:
CLEAN, CLUTTER, AND COLOR

Think of the three C's as you go through the house with your sellers.

Clean

Have you ever gone to see someone else's listing and when you walked across the kitchen floor your foot stuck to it? Well, I've been there too. When it comes to your listings, however, they are going to be clean.

Clean houses are more appealing. They look better, and buyers will assume that a clean home is better cared for. Many buyers will walk out of a dirty listing without even considering what's underneath the dirt because they feel so uncomfortable. You need to be honest with your sellers and point out areas and rooms that need attention. This includes cleaning the top of the refrigerator, scouring the stove, shampooing the carpets if necessary, wiping away all the cobwebs in the corners of the ceilings, really cleaning the baths, and much more.

Sometimes as we are living in a house, we tend to let such things go. We say to ourselves, "I really do need to get around to that." When sellers decide to sell the house, then it is time to "get around to it."

When it comes to sellers who do not know what clean is, I feel it is really your job to show them the problems you are talking about in a nice way. I'll never forget showing a seller with four children what needed to be done under her kitchen cupboards where the cookie crumbs and sticky Koolaid had been spilled everywhere. You may be thinking, "You really showed her?" You better believe it, and she took it in a great way. She wanted to get her house sold so she could join her husband in another city where he had already started his new job. Motivation is the key! Sellers who do not want to move would probably object or be offended, but not those who want to sell and want their money.

Remember, its not what you say, but how you say it that counts. I believe, just like the doctor, attorney, or accountant, that we must think of our clients first, do our job, and tell them. If you are worried about a tough problem, use my analogy of the doctor who has to tell the patient something difficult. Because the doctor cares, he or she discusses it with the patient instead of simply holding back or not saying anything. Think of the tough job doctors have when they have to tell patients they are dying. Thinking of that has given me great courage many times to tell sellers that their home smells like cats, or even worse. Once I had to tell a seller that there was a smell of human urine in her home, and the doctor story really gave me courage. And if I can tell someone his or her home smells like human urine, you can tell your sellers *anything!* It isn't what you say, it's how you say it and when you say it. Timing is also very important.

By the way, I told the woman about her problem by sitting her down at the kitchen table, holding her hand, and talking about how doctors have to tell patients things sometimes that are difficult to say. I went on and told her that what I needed to share with her was very difficult for me to say, but if I didn't tell her no one else would.

I told her about the problem after she had signed my listing agreement. Also, remember in my listing presentation I ask my sellers to give me their commitment to *Stage* their home, and she had already said she would before I listed the house. It worked. We took care of the problem over the weekend before my company tour, before the sign went up, and before the buyers started coming through on Monday. The house sold immediately, and I will never forget the feeling inside when at closing she said how glad she was I had the strength to tell her of the "problem" because she really did need to sell!

Clutter

You've heard of the "lived-in look." Usually that means clutter. We all have clutter in our homes. There is nothing wrong with that— unless you are trying to sell your house. Remember to teach your sellers the following:

> **The way you live in a home and the way you sell a home are two different things.**

I sincerely believe that we all have a right to live in our homes any way we want. But when our homes come on the market for sale that is something different. The public is now going to be coming through the house, and now it is a product for sale on the market.

Clutter makes it difficult for a purchaser to *mentally move into* a home. Most of our homes come on the market with simply too much stuff in them. Have your sellers pack up extra things that they really don't need while they are selling and put them away. I have had many sellers rent storage space or store these things in a basement. If they cannot rent a storage space or if they do not have a basement, they can pack their extra things in boxes and stack them *neatly* in one corner of the garage.

So, look for too many books, knickknacks, plants, or even too many pieces of furniture in a room. Tell your sellers the truth: "Buyers can't mentally move all of their things into your home until we put some of your things away. Psychologists also tell us, Mr. and Mrs. Seller, that no one will buy a home until he or she mentally moves in. We have got to pack up some of your things."

Color

Look at the color scheme of the house from room to room. Is there a common theme or is there a different and contrasting color in every room? Is there a different color of carpet in every room? This can really give a house a chopped-up feeling. It can make the home seem smaller than it really is. Are the walls painted the same off-white throughout the house and is the same soft color of carpet used throughout? If they are, this gives the home more of a flowing feeling and can help it seem even more spacious than it is. These are things to keep in mind if it looks like the sellers need to do any painting or replace the floor coverings.

Remember, *Staging* usually doesn't mean spending a lot of money. So don't be confused by my comments about painting and carpeting. Sometimes a home or condominium desperately needs paint or carpet. If the sellers can afford it, great! Recommend it as we are discussing here. However, there are many times that sellers simply can't afford it or refuse to consider it. The property can still be *Staged* by spending little or no money. Cleaning the carpet or washing walls can work wonders. Even spot cleaning the carpets helps. Cleaning spots on walls, patching or touching up the paint is easy and can add a lot too. *Stage* it the best you can. Every little bit helps.

As an extra service to get the listing and to help your sellers I suggest that you offer to go with them to help pick out the right color of paint or carpet. They could pick one that is actually worse than the one they had before! Be involved— it really does pay. Not only will offering this help you get the listing, but this way you can be sure they put in the right color, and this will help you sell the house and help you get paid.

When it comes to paint, remind your sellers that a gallon of paint, on sale at the hardware store, is usually less than the cost of a carton of cigarettes. I've never had a seller say no to buying paint when you put it in those terms. Even one gallon can work miracles in painting a small bath or a child's room. (Most buyers just don't buy homes with purple bedrooms or baths.) Outside one gallon works wonders on the trim, the front door, or shutters to give a crisp new look.

If you are working with a seller who doesn't want to replace worn carpet and says, "We'll just let the buyers do it when they move in," remind your sellers of my saying, which I whole-heartedly believe:

> **Buyers only know what they see, not the way it's going to be!**

I developed that saying out of the experience of *Staging* the For Sale by Owner I've mentioned earlier, before I had the name on the dotted line. The best friends who bought the house couldn't imagine that the house could look so good. It is crucial that you take the time to educate your sellers that most buyers have very little imagination. Therefore, even if your sellers are willing to give an allowance for carpet, most buyers cannot imagine another carpet in the home, and they will probably keep looking at other homes that are for sale instead of purchasing this one. This is why I don't recommend allowances for listings. Also, many real estate agents only remember what they see, not the way it's going to be, and they hold the power to decide whether or not they want to bring buyers to see your listings. I always think it's best to paint or recarpet *before* any agent or buyer is allowed to see your listing.

If you are wondering what color of carpet to recommend I know that you already know. I believe in you, and I am going to prove to you that you already know. Would you recommend that the seller put in wild yellow? Of course not. How about shocking blue? No. How about black? Never. How about pure white? Never. Well, how about "real estate beige?" Yes, of course! See, I told you, you know. A nice beige will go well with most purchasers' furnishings.

It is important that you discuss colors, paint, and carpet during the pricing section of your Detailed Report because they can definitely affect the list price. I also would never tell my sellers that they will get back the cost of replacing the carpet dollar for dollar, but I do tell them that it could be the thing that will help them sell their home.

What about color in furniture and fixtures? Is there a green and purple plaid afghan on the blue-striped couch? If so, have the sellers pack the afghan. Are there three colors of towels in the bathroom? Ask the sellers to use towels that match, or suggest they find some new ones on sale that will complement the bath and can be used in their new home after this one sells. Pay attention to colors and color schemes in each room as well as the whole house.

Color is very important in marketing a home and is one of the important three C's.

THE KEY: DO IT NOW!

When I first started *Staging* homes, years ago, I would sometimes suggest things to my sellers that somehow they never quite got done. You know what I mean. You list the property, then three months later you are still waiting for the sellers to clear off the dining room table or put away all the knickknacks on the hutch. That is not the way it should ever be, so I came up with a way that really works to get them to do it immediately.

First, I started to think about *Staging* the house and how I was really *Staging* merchandise or, as in Hollywood, the set. I then began to think of myself as a director with the house being the set and the sellers being the actors. Think about Hollywood—they *Stage* every set to look great and sometimes even to look bad. Of course we want our sets to look the very best they can. Consider the audience as well. Who are they? They are the buyers and the other agents coming through. So be proud and confident, because you are the director!

Second, I always go over these words with my sellers before we start to *Stage* the house: *list, sell, move, and pack.* I simply ask the sellers the following questions as we start to *Stage*: "You have entrusted your *listing* to me because you expect me to *sell* your home, isn't that correct?" Of course they say, "yes." Then I ask, "And when we *sell*, that means you'll need to *move*, isn't that correct, also?" They say, "yes," again. "And when you *move*, you'll need to *pack*! Right?" They say, "yes," again. And now you finish by saying, "So all we are going to do is to *pack* you up early." Sellers buy that because it is true. It works. Try it.

I also thought about my daughter and what I have her do if I want her to clean out her room, or go through her closet to sort out clothes or toys she no longer uses. What do you do when you go through your closets or garage to give or throw things away? We all make piles of some kind don't we? So, as simple as it sounds (simple is always best) I had my sellers start to make piles. It works every time. My sellers have been making piles for years. I also want you to know that I have never had a seller refuse to make piles. Why? Because I educated them from the beginning about how important *Staging* really is. By the time we get to the piles they just say, "OK, Barb, tell us what to do."

As you go through each room, ask your sellers to pile all the things you suggest they pack up in the middle of the room. Then when you leave, the sellers can just put these things in boxes, pack them into storage or the garage, and they are ready for the move. Do this room by room. This is what you told them in the beginning when you first talked about the *Staging* process when you said, "Let me tell you how I work." Now, a lot of real estate salespeople smile when I tell them to do this, but I really do use this technique because it works! No sellers are going to leave a pile of their things lying in the middle of the room if they want you marketing the house. Set your standards, and they will match them and do what you ask. You and I are the doctors in our own field of real estate when it comes to *Staging*.

Stay in control by having them take care of most things *right then* while you are there and can help or advise. Do everything you can together with your sellers at that time, and you won't have to worry about those problems later. The only things that you don't do immediately with your sellers are the projects that can't be completed right away, like painting a room or fixing the broken dishwasher.

As you go through a home with your sellers and you come up with things that cannot be done right then, simply make a list as you go. Be sure that everything that cannot be done right away goes on the list! That is very important. I've never had a seller tell me "no" at this point.

Go room by room with your sellers. Have them make piles in every room and make a list of the things they need to do that cannot be done immediately. Later in chapter 15, I will show you how to be sure that your sellers get everything on the list done and the piles put away. *Staging* is where the money is, and you can have fun doing it, too! It really does pay.

The following are photos of rooms before and after they were *Staged* (Figures 13–1 to 13–3). You can see for yourself what a difference it makes.

I suggest that you reread this important section if you are at all unsure about how you can actually get people to make piles and pack up some of their things early. If you educate your sellers from the first contact until it's time to *Stage* the property then they will *want* this extra service from you. If you follow the steps I outlined your sellers will make piles and complete their list because they need you and trust you.

Before I end this chapter I would like to discuss my "Tips for Selling." These are specific to the inside of the home. I will share my tips for the outside of the home in the next chapter.

TIPS FOR SELLING

Say the following phrase to your sellers as soon as you start *Staging* their home, and you will have all the cooperation you need:

> **Start packing, because with me as your agent, you will be moving soon.**

This really hits home, and they understand what you are talking about. Then you can take them step by step and have them clear, clean, and pack up any of their belongings to make their home look better.

Now I would like to share some specific tips on *Staging* the sellers' property.

Tip 1: Clear Away All Unnecessary Objects Throughout House

This includes objects on end tables, dressers, coffee tables, counters, and any other furniture throughout the entire house.

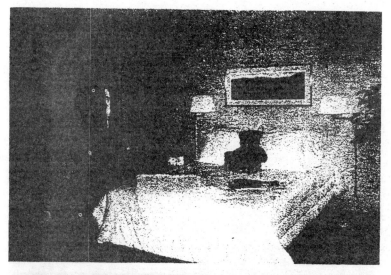

FIGURE 13-1

This doesn't mean you strip the house bare. But you do want your sellers to keep little ornaments and knickknacks limited to groups of one, three, or five. Have them pack away all extras.

For example, let's say the sellers have fifteen little Hummel figures they have collected over the years on the end table in the living room. Ask them to pack almost all of them. They might want to leave out one or three. But, if they are worried about

FIGURE 13-2

any of them breaking, have them put them all away. As for magazines scattered on the coffee table in the living room, either remove them or stack them up, but don't leave out any more than three. Also remove the extra pillows, afghans, newspapers, and various other items from the living room, den, kitchen, or any other main room in the house. Mantels should also be cleared off, leaving only one, three, or five small items. Remember, you need to create room for future buyers to move in their own possessions mentally as they view your listing.

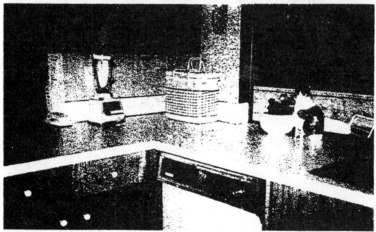

FIGURE 13-3

Tip 2: Rearrange Dining Room Furniture to Create More Space

If the sellers are using extra leaves in their dining room table, have them take them out and put them in a closet. This will make a dining room look bigger. If it is a huge dining room, however, it is better to leave in the table sections. That will show purchasers how nicely a large table fits in the room. Also, put any extra dining room chairs away. Again, this will create space.

If you can't move the chairs to another room, put them in the garage. I've had lots of dining room chairs sitting in garages in my listings, but it helped get the house sold!

If they have a hutch or a buffet in the dining room, have them clear any excess items from it, including anything that might be stored on top of it. Also, anything valuable should be taken out of the hutch and packed away. "Out of sight means out of mind."

Tip 3: Clear Away Unnecessary Objects from Kitchen Counter Tops

"What can you live without?" is the key question you should always ask your sellers. Also ask your sellers, "What, in the kitchen, haven't you used for the last three months?" You'll have reactions like, "Well, let's see, I haven't used the coffee pot for a while because we quit drinking coffee." Or, "Oh, I used to bake so much bread, but I don't do that anymore so I really don't need the mixer." Have them put those things in a pile on the kitchen table.

While you are in the kitchen, have them clear away messages, pictures, comics, and so forth, from the front of the refrigerator. Many times, sellers have drawings the little ones have made in kindergarten or the grandchildren have made in school. Ask them to clear those things off. You might say, "Sally, can we just pick the very favorite picture that your son did? Let's put it up, and put the others away." This works very effectively. Also watch for the tops of refrigerators. These can be collect-alls and need to be clean and clutter free.

Remind your sellers also that a sparse, clean kitchen, one in which you can see almost all the counter tops, makes a kitchen look bigger and helps a potential purchaser mentally move his or her own things into the kitchen. If the kitchen is cluttered with dirty dishes in a dirty sink, or things are strewn all over the window ledge, or the counters are covered with appliances and crumbs, then purchasers are going to have some trouble mentally moving in. So, advise them to keep the sink clean, the counter tops clear, the appliances clean, and to keep the whole kitchen neat as long as the house is on the market. This means *every single day*, because you never know when the right agent with the right buyers will walk through the door.

Have them move such items as soap dispensers, scouring pads, and dish drainers underneath the sink. Clear away all but one or two items from the window ledge. A small plant and a knickknack or two might look nice there, but not lots of items. Ask your sellers to be tough on themselves and give up what they can truly live without. Once they get in the swing of things, sellers usually start to be harder on themselves than you or I would be. Now it's starting to get fun.

Tip 4: Remove All Unnecessary Items in Bathrooms

Most bathrooms have too many things scattered all over the counter, around the tub and shower, and all over the back of the commode. Ask your sellers to put those things in a cabinet, under the sink, or pack them up early. Have the sellers put away all but their most needed cosmetics, brushes, perfumes, and so forth, and then ask them to keep those necessary items in one small group on the counter at all times. I also ask sellers to put away any small garbage cans in the bathroom or put them behind the toilet where you cannot see them. Another thing is to keep the lid down on the toilet while on the market. This way it does not look like we are marketing garbage or toilets. It may sound funny, but it all subtly affects buyers when they look at a home.

You can really straighten up a bathroom if you tuck all the necessary toiletries into a basket or set them on a tray. Baskets, bowls, and trays are great for organizing things in the bathroom, the kitchen, and on desks or dressers. Most people already have baskets and trays, and everybody has a bowl. However, you might suggest that your sellers buy some baskets or trays if they don't already have them.

Coordinate towels, limiting them to one or two colors that match the room. If the sellers have a matching set, use those towels. If they don't have a matching set or nice collection of towels, then suggest they buy some. A good way to phrase this would be to say, "You know, it is really a small investment, so how about going down to the department store and just buying one or two sets of towels? Then you can use them in your new home when you move."

While you are in the bathroom, check again for any problems, like weak flooring where bath water has spilled. If possible, things like that need to be taken care of before the house goes on the market, or they must be disclosed in the listing agreement. Check behind the toilets and under the sink for leaks. Check the shower and tub for mildew, cracks, or bad grout.

The bathroom is one room where cleanliness is crucial. Be honest with your sellers if you see anything that needs attention, such as counters, sinks, toilets, shower stalls, mirrors, soap scum, mold, and so forth.

Tip 5: Rearrange the Furniture, If Necessary

Sometimes we just put too much furniture in our rooms. That may be fine for living, but it's not good for selling. In the living room, for instance, your sellers may have too many chairs, which creates a feeling of less space for the potential purchaser. You want to create just the opposite impression, and removing a chair or an ottoman can really help. Focus a lot of your attention on those main "emotional rooms" when you are *Staging* the property—the living room, kitchen, and master bedroom. You want those rooms to look sharp because those are the rooms on which most buyers will focus.

You may face the sellers' question of "Where do we put the extra furniture?" There are certain areas in a home that I do not worry about extensively. One of them is the garage. Put extra chairs in the garage. The garage, basement, attic, or storage room are perfect places to store extra furniture and all the other items you are removing from the main rooms in the house. Other sellers may choose or need to rent a storage unit in a self-storage warehouse. Sometimes, if there are too many chairs in a living room or dining room, we can take one or more of them and put them in a bedroom that is fairly empty. Try moving pieces of furniture from one room to another. Sometimes just rearranging the furniture creates more space without removing anything.

If you just can't find any place to put extra furniture or boxes and there is a third or fourth bedroom that is not in use, you can sacrifice that one room and neatly fill it full of boxes or extra furniture. Although this is not ideal, it does work, because the important rooms for selling are still *Staged* to look great.

Tip 6: Take Down or Rearrange Pictures or Other Objects on the Wall

We've all seen the phenomenon where, for instance, there may be forty posters on the walls in a child's room. Have the sellers take most of these down, and if necessary, patch the holes and touch up the paint. If your sellers don't, the purchasers are going to think, "Oh my, I'm going to have to patch all these holes and paint the walls." So, if the sellers do this ahead of time, it will help tremendously in selling the house. You might suggest the parents let the kids keep up one or two of their favorite posters, but no more than that.

Clutter on the wall can happen to many rooms, so be sure to check for too many pictures in the living room, family room, and even baths. Remember to tell them that you're just going to help them pack up early to help get the house sold.

Tip 7: Paint Any Rooms that Need It

Painting is not something that you should suggest very often. If the paint in one or many rooms is in bad shape or is a bad color, however, then you must decide which rooms need painting or repapering and suggest it. Painting is one of the cheapest things sellers can do to improve their home. Off-white is definitely the best color. Remember that whites have different shades or tones to them. Some whites have blue shades; some have green, yellow, or pink tints. So pick a safe color that works with the carpet and floor coverings in your sellers' home. Off-white is always the safest way to go, because most furniture will work with off-white colors, and that makes it easier for the potential purchasers to mentally move in.

If you come across rooms with wild or dark colors, suggest that your sellers repaint them. You and I know that some sellers have some far-out colors, such as navy blue walls in the bedroom or a wacky flower design on the wallpaper in the kitchen. That was great for living in the home but not for selling it. Put those rooms down on the list for painting and papering. If the walls in halls have been marked or scarred, have the sellers clean, paint, or touch them up as well.

Painting and wallpapering is not always necessary, but it is one of the least expensive things that can be done to make a home look better than the competition.

Tip 8: Clean Carpets or Drapes

The difference clean carpets and drapes can make is well worth the expense of having the drapes dry cleaned and the carpets steamed cleaned. It really is a small cost of selling a home.

Sometimes the drapes need to be removed altogether. For example, the drapes may be so dark and heavy that they overpower the room. If there is a sheer drape underneath, you can say, "Mr. and Mrs. Seller, let's take down these overdrapes. They are a heavy brocade and they are making the room darker than we need for selling. But leave the sheers, and you will still have some privacy at night."

Now, you may be thinking, "I can't get my sellers to do that. They love those brocade drapes." You *can* do it. Be confident. Remember you are the expert (the director) who they respect. Sellers want your opinions so they can get their equity. They are not going to be there much longer. They are moving, remember? So, when the seller says, "Oh, but I really enjoy those drapes," just say, "That's OK. You're moving, remember. You are not going to be here anymore!" (Besides that, if the sellers take them down now and pack them away before purchasers start to look at the property, the sellers could keep them because they would not be included in the sale of the house.) Whenever your sellers don't like a change you are suggesting, just remind them they are moving. It works like magic!

Tip 9: Clean the Windows

Dirty windows are difficult to see through, and they give a home a poor image. I find that most sellers plan to clean their windows anyway. But sometimes you'll meet people who just forget about it. Remind them! Put it on their list and have them get it done.

Tip 10: Take Care of Any Odors

If there is a unique problem such as odors from a pet, cooking, or smoke, you must address this. This can be a sensitive area. But, as the expert, you need to tell your sellers about such problems.

One way you can handle this is to use an example that is the opposite of their problem. For example, let's say you are working with someone who has pets, but they don't smoke. You could say to them, "You don't smoke, do you?" (Be sure they don't before you ask this question.) They will answer, "No, I don't." Then ask them, "Have you ever been in someone's home where the people who lived there smoked? Did you notice how you could pick up on that smell in the carpets, the drapes, and even in the people's clothes?" Usually they will say something like, "Yes, and I can't stand it. I can't even breathe when I'm in a smoker's house." Then say, "Well, you know, Sally and John, there are a lot of qualified purchasers out there who do not have pets such as your beautiful cat (use the pet's name). Now, you are accustomed to the aroma of your own pets, but purchasers who do not have any animals may be very sensitive to those aromas. So, we need to do something about that." Use the word "aroma" when you are talking about the seller's situation. It's safer that way. But you can refer to the other people's problems as "smells," as I did earlier. Use a situation that does not apply to them to explain the way others may feel coming into their home.

Then recommend they ventilate their home by opening windows on opposite ends of the house. They might also try an air cleaner/deodorizer machine. In many cases, the carpet needs to be cleaned to remove certain smells. Whatever the situation is, be sure to address it.

When it comes to pet odors, check your local pet store for the latest in products that can help the problem of pet smells or eliminate them completely. Some of the latest products really do work and don't smell worse than the problem, like they used to. Also, gift stores now carry potpourri that you put out in a small basket, and they really smell delightful. They have been oiled with a wonderful fragrance so you do not have to light them like a candle, which could be dangerous.

If you don't tell your sellers about an odor problem, then who will? This can make a big difference in the length of time it takes you to sell their house. As you know, it can even influence the actual sale price of a home.

Tip 11: Clean the Fireplace

If the fireplace is full of dirty ashes or needs some work, then add that to the list. Ask your sellers to leave the fireplace screen closed during showings. If the screen has rusted, have them spray it with a black paint from the hardware store. Most hardware stores have a spray paint that is heat resistant, and will not melt or come off as the new buyer builds fires in the future. If it is summertime, and the fireplace is cleaned out, put a plant in front of the fireplace to add some greenery to the room. Have your sellers do whatever they can to improve its appearance.

If the outside front of the fireplace has soot on it, have your sellers clean it off. Have them test a small, out-of-the-way area on the fireplace with oven cleaner or soot remover. I have seen this take off the soot many times successfully, without damaging the fireplace. Another idea for dark fireplaces, or fireplaces where nothing seems to be able to get rid of the soot, is to have your sellers paint the face of the fireplace with a brick paint from the hardware store. There are paints especially made for bricks that will not come off and it will make the fireplace look better and bigger as well. Use semigloss, white brick paint. It almost seems like a miracle in the right situation.

If there is any damage at all to the fireplace be sure your seller fixes it or discloses it. One or the other must be done.

You will be amazed at the difference these tips can make in a house. Always look for opportunities to improve the showing condition of your sellers' house. The better the home looks, the better the price it can command on the market!

You can also use these tips as a marketing tool. I keep a typed set of them in my *Career Book* and *Marketing Portfolio*. Sellers love it! These are general tips that can apply to any house. Use the tips for *Staging* the inside of your sellers' home whenever and wherever you find them helpful. They really do work.[1]

Now, let's head for the great outdoors.

[1]Please see the Appendix for complete details on how to order your copy of the Barb Schwarz "How to Prepare Your Home for Sale...So It Sells" video to show your sellers. This hour long video will help you help sellers prepare their homes for sale.

14

Staging™ *the Property: The Outside Story*

In this chapter you will learn

1. How to help your sellers see the outside of their homes from the buyers' point of view.
2. More of my "tips for selling" for the outside of the property.
3. Some general pointers on showing a house at its best.

The way a home looks from the curb may determine how many potential purchasers will look at the inside of it. So, the *Staging* of your sellers' homes on the outside is just as important as the *Staging* of the interior.

POWER OF FIRST IMPRESSIONS

The inside of a home may be where most people spend most of their time, but it is the outside of the home that many times attracts purchasers. This is known as curb appeal— how good the property looks from the street. As real estate agents, you and I know that often the first thing a showing agent does is to park the car with the buyers across the street from a seller's home. If peeling paint or falling gutters completely turn off the purchaser, the property has just taken a giant step backward— no matter how good the interior of the house looks. So, it is just as important to prepare the outside of the house as the inside.

THE BUYERS' POINT OF VIEW

One of the most effective ways to get your sellers' cooperation when *Staging* the outside of their home is to take them across the street, and have them look at their house. Many people never look at the outside of their house objectively after they buy it. They walk out of the house in the morning, get in a car, and drive off to work without looking back. When they return home, they whisk into the garage without even looking up or looking at how their home really appears. We are all this way. Some days I come home, and the drive is so routine, it seems like I can't even remember how I got home.

So, take your sellers across the street and say, "Look back at your house, Mr. and Mrs. Seller, and I want you to think like a buyer. Tell me what you see." The sellers will usually stand there a second. Then, all of a sudden, they will get tough on themselves. They'll see things they haven't seen for years. For instance, they might say, "Gosh, I didn't know that gutter was coming down." When they say these things, add them to their list of things to be repaired. Or they might say, "Wow, that front door sure looks bad. I guess it'll need a new coat of paint." From this viewpoint they usually can't help but notice how overgrown the plants are. They'll say something like, "The rhododendrons have grown so high, I can't even see the den window."

Now, if the house is overgrown by plants and the seller doesn't bring it up, I do. "Do you see how the right side of your house is buried behind the two very large plants, Mr. and Mrs. Seller? In fact, aren't those your master bedroom and den windows behind the plants?" The sellers both answer, "yes." "Well, Mr. and Mrs. Seller, I noticed that inside those two rooms of your house it was darker than in the other rooms. Now, I don't think the problem is with the rooms at all. I think the rooms are darker inside because the plants have grown so large outside they are preventing light from flooding into those rooms. Wouldn't you say that is correct?" Again your sellers will answer, "yes."

This is when I teach my theory of, "you can't sell it if you can't see it." Learn this saying. How can you sell something if you can't see it? It only makes good sense! Teach this theory to your sellers, and I promise it will make good sense to them as well. But you must take them across the street to get the full impact. Telling them in their living room about their overgrown plants, which are outside, or even telling them on their front porch, usually won't work as well for you. Take them across the street. This really gives you the power you need. Teach your sellers that light homes are really in demand these days. I don't know anywhere in the country, after teaching my class in literally almost every state in the union, where light isn't "in." Today's buyers always ask us to show them light and bright homes. You need to share this with your sellers so they under-stand what today's buyers want.

Also, another powerful thing to share with sellers is that, "plants are like kids." I think that when we have them they are so little and cute, then they get just about right and then plants— like kids— get so big that some of us don't know how to take care of them anymore. This is very effective with the sellers who tell you they planted the tree that is now grown over the entire top of the roof.

Now, we cannot trim our kids, but we sure can trim the plants to let in more light. We don't usually have to cut the entire plant down to the ground, although sometimes it is necessary. Most of the time trimming up the branches or trimming the plant in certain places will let more light into the room, but the plant will still look good. It works. Tell your sellers as you add it to their list that you will help them establish how much or how little to trim. Remember the key is to let more light into the rooms and to let the house be shown from the curb at its best.

Sometimes you will get sign calls on a listing, and the buyer will tell you on the phone that it is overpriced. One common reason this happens is because the shrubbery is overgrown, and the buyer cannot see the house. They think it is smaller than it may be and conclude that it is overpriced. The real fact is, "you can't sell it if you can't see it!"

When you take sellers across the street, several great things happen. First of all, they get to be the "bad guy" criticizing the house and you don't have to. If you were to talk to them about the outside of their home when you were on the inside, however, it would not mean nearly as much.

Second, taking them across the street is wonderful because it gives so much more perspective, and the strings are really cut from the property by walking the sellers across the street. Usually, when you ask how long it has been since your sellers looked at their home like a buyer, they will say, "Not since the day I bought it," or "never."

Let the sellers talk and name all that they can about what they see and what they think they need to do with the property to get it ready for sale. Bring up things you see that they missed when they finish talking. Remember, the first time you went to see the property you should have sat across the street and really looked at the house to figure these things out so you know how to guide your sellers when it is time to *Stage* the house and make their list to get things done. Together, write down everything on the list as you talk about the actual things that need to be done on the outside of the property.

Also walk all the way around the outside of the house, continuing the list as you go. Keep your eyes open to anything and everything you think needs to be done, and talk about it with your seller openly. Don't hold back on anything. You owe it to your sellers and yourself to bring up anything you see, even if it may be difficult. Discuss the two-by-fours piled by the house, and ask the sellers where they can be moved to and put away. Have your sellers move the pots filled with the dead plants off of the deck or patio. Ask your sellers to move the old worn-out patio furniture if it is cluttering up the back yard. All of these things detract from showing the property to potential purchasers.

Staging the outside of the property is so crucial. It is just as crucial as the inside, and making the list with your sellers is extremely important. Then you want to make sure that the list gets done and everything gets put away. We will talk about how to be sure that it does get done in the next chapter.

TIPS ON SELLING FOR OUTSIDE OF PROPERTY

Just like the tips I gave you in the previous chapter on the inside of the home, these pointers work wonders with the outside of someone's home. Use them with your sellers because they really do work. Share them from the very beginning in your *Career Book* and then again in your *Marketing Portfolio* as you work with your sellers. By the time you come to actually *Stage* the house, your sellers will already know the general theory of what you are going to have them do. But remember, only zero in on the actual items, one by one, after they have signed your listing agreement. In other words, trimming the plants and bushes outside the house is noted on the "Tips for Selling" list, and you should talk about the idea during your listing presentation if it fits the situation; but you don't actually show them which bush or where to trim it until the sellers have signed the listing.

Tip 1: Move All Garbage Cans, Discarded Wood Scraps, and Extra Building Materials

Go around the perimeter of the house with the sellers to make sure everything is cleaned out of the yard. Have the sellers put these things into the garage, or take them to the dump! Most of us as individual homeowners have some of these things around the outside of our homes. But remember, "the way we live in a home and the way we sell a home are two different things." Add all the things to the list that the sellers are going to do.

Tip 2: Check the Gutters and the Roof

Take the time to look at the roof and gutters, and look for and discuss any possible problems such as dry rot, moss, debris, leaks, and so forth. Have your sellers clean out the gutters and make sure that they are securely attached to the house all the way around. If at all possible, the sellers should fix any problems such as a leaky roof. If they do have a problem, and they are not going to repair it, you must disclose that in the listing agreement.

Tip 3: Check for Termites or Other Insect Problems

Some sellers can have problems with termites or other types of insects in a home. So, keep your eye out for obvious signs of infestation. It is always better to be safe than sorry even if it means your sellers have to do some extra repair work to take care of a "bug" problem. Also, nothing chases away potential buyers faster than roaches or other creepy crawlers. If you spot any evidence of unwanted house guests, have the sellers call an exterminator and get it done now, as well as repair any damaged areas.

Tip 4: Look at the Bushes and Trees

One of the best phrases I have ever developed to use with sellers is the following:

> **We can't sell it if we can't see it.**

That is the truth! So, have the sellers trim back any bushes or shrubbery that is obscuring the house from view. Tall plants not only make it difficult for potential purchasers to see your sellers' home, they block light from the windows. Suggest to the sellers that they trim back the bushes and prune the trees. Sometimes, trees are so overgrown the sellers need to cut away the lower branches so purchasers can see the front of the house. It's called "skirting the tree," and it works like a charm. Have your sellers remove any dead plants or shrubs. Sometimes you work with sellers who have not yet removed a couple of plants that died the year before. It's just one of those things they never got around to doing. If you see any dying or dead foliage, point it out to the sellers, and put it on the list for them to do.

Tip 5: Weed and Bark All Planting Areas, and Groom and Fertilize the Lawn

Many yards can use a little sprucing up before they go on the market. Be honest with your sellers about what you see and how they can improve it. The investment is small or it can be done with just a little extra time and effort. If beauty bark is widely used in your area of the country, then have your sellers put fresh bark in their planting areas. Different parts of the country use different ground cover mulches, so whatever it is, have your sellers add a fresh layer. Or ask them to at least till the ground in the planting areas, so there is fresh dirt and no weeds. The lawn also needs to be kept cut, and a little fertilizer is a small investment to really make a lawn look sharp. This is true for vacant properties that you list as well.

Tip 6: Clear Patios or Decks of All Small Items

Move extra planters, empty flower pots, charcoal, grills, toys, anything like that, into the garage or storage shed. If it is summertime, and they are going to use the barbecue grill, at least put it in one corner of the patio or deck. If it is wintertime, have your sellers put it away in the garage.

One of my pet peeves, which my friends kid me about, is seeing dead or dying potted plants that people refuse to throw away. We all do it, and you know the kind I mean. They have two short sticks coming out of the pot with three faded leaves just barely surviving. For example, people tend to keep poinsettias. Do you still have a poinsettia from the Christmas season before last? Yes, I thought so. Or at least we all seem to hang onto plants that are continually on their last leg. It's the middle of August, and there is a poinsettia, with its red foil wrap, sitting on the deck, half with us and half gone. Have your sellers clear away all those things. By the way, most of us keep these sick plants for two reasons: hope and guilt. Your sellers will love you because when you talk to them about the sick plants, they will be so happy to throw them out, as you have just saved them from feeling guilty anymore. Here is how I do this. I just look at the sickest plant they have, then I look at the sellers, back to the plant again, and then I say, "I don't think it's going to make the move, do you?" The sellers laugh and say, "No, Barb, you are right. It will probably croak in the moving van." Have them take it to the garbage right then. This works great for plants on the inside of the house as well as the outside.

Keep flower pots to a minimum and full of live beautiful flowers, if it is springtime or summer. If it is winter, put all of them away. Keep decks and patios cleared of lots of small things. And the same goes for the front yard and back yard. The more things there are to distract the eye, the harder it is to sell the property.

Tip 7: Check the Paint Condition of the House— Especially the Front Door and Trim

Here is where curb appeal really works! The paint job is one of the first things a potential buyer notices. So, if the paint is peeling off the house, a number one priority would be to try to have them repaint the whole house. But let's say the sellers can't afford to paint the entire house. Those circumstances come up for all of us from time to time. Ask them if they could just paint the front door. I haven't met a seller yet who couldn't afford one gallon of paint for the front door and its trim. Remember, after all, one gallon of paint on sale at the hardware store is less than fifteen dollars. I have yet to run into sellers who were motivated to move, no matter how poor they were, who would not buy a gallon of paint when asked in that fashion.

In an earlier chapter I suggested that you offer the service of helping them pick out the color of paint if they are going to paint their home. If you offer this when you first meet them, this will help you get the listing because people love to have your advice and expertise. If you are unsure of color, I suggest that you go to where new homes are being built and look at the colors that the builders are using. After all, they are in the business of building homes to make money for a living, and they usually know the best and latest colors to use. Then suggest some of these colors to your sellers. Also, paint brochures are another source of excellent ideas for paint colors—especially the ones that show pictures of homes already painted.

Check the front door for any damage. If there are claw marks from a dog or a cat, have those repaired and painted. Is the doorknob working properly? Does the doorbell work? Your goal is to assure that the house makes a good first impression.

Tip 8: Finish Any Unfinished Projects

If a pile of lumber is lying in the yard because the sellers haven't finished putting the last planks on a new deck, have the sellers make that a priority project. This rule applies to the inside as well. It applies to any project that has not yet been completed. If your sellers started it before they ever met you but never finished it, now is the time. That can make a tremendous difference to a purchaser, and can earn the sellers, at times, a higher selling price. The opposite is also true. That's why it's important to educate your sellers that most buyers are not interested in taking over someone else's project, and that decreases the total number of possible buyers and usually increases selling time and can also ultimately reduce the selling price. I think it's actually better, if possible, to remove what has been started rather than list a property with a partially completed project. Of course, many times that is impossible, so have the sellers get the project done.

Tip 9: Go Completely around the Whole Property

For your information, protection, and for *Staging*, I suggest that you walk around the whole property with your sellers, or without them if they are physically unable. If it is dark outside I suggest you return during the daylight hours. This way you can be sure there are no surprises that the sellers forgot to tell you about, such as an abandoned well, a junk pile, any building materials or firewood piled against the house (a red flag for inspectors!), or anything else that looks suspicious or unattractive.

These are my "Tips for Selling" on *Staging* the outside of a home. Do take the time necessary to go over all of them and to go through the whole house with your sellers. It will pay off in countless ways for you and your sellers.

TIPS FOR SHOWING A HOME

In addition to *Staging* the house, you can also teach your sellers a few simple ideas to help them show their house at its best for potential purchasers. Share these pointers with your sellers.

For all of your sellers I am going to suggest you teach them three important words when it comes to showings: *lights, music,* and *action.* I will explain each of these in detail subsequently. I always want my sellers to know that I expect them to have lights, music, and action when it comes to *Staging* a home. Ask each of your sellers about where they buy things that they need such as their favorite department store, grocery store, drug store, or even where they would buy a car. Do these places normally have lights on, music playing, and marketing action as they set the *Stage* for selling? Of course, they do! That is because it is conducive to buying, and that is what we want for our sellers and their homes. The very same rules apply. We want to appeal to the emotions of the buyer during all showings. Remember that agents, appraisers, and inspectors are people with emotions, too. These people are crucial to the sale and closing of your listing. Lights, music, and action help in every situation in a very professional way. Educate your sellers on this important point so that your listing will be in the best showing condition possible at all times.

Tip 1: Have Your Sellers Leave on Certain Lights at All Times During the Day

Show them which ones, because they often don't know. I recommend they always leave the lights on in the darkest spots in the house. For example, let's say they have a hallway that is very dark; there is no skylight, and the light from the bedroom windows doesn't quite make it into the hallway. Ask them to spend the few pennies it takes to leave a few lights on in those dark spaces.

If your sellers say to you, "That is going to cost too much," ask them, "How much will it cost you if you don't sell your home?" That really helps them understand why it is necessary. The extra pennies they will spend on electricity are insignificant compared with the equity they will be getting from their home.

Tip 2: Have Your Sellers Turn on All Lamps During Showings

Educate all your sellers to go from room to room and turn on every lamp and light in the house for a showing. It's the same as when you go to a store to buy a new piece of clothing. If that store has done its *Staging* correctly, the lighting makes the clothes look terrific.

Tip 3: Leave All Curtains, Drapes, and Blinds Open for Showings

Again, good lighting is imperative. It is good to have your sellers leave their window treatments open all day, especially if everyone who lives in the home is gone during the day because no one would be there to open them for an unexpected showing. Also show your sellers how far open to pull the drapes. When it comes to blinds, a lot of people tip their vertical blinds upward or downward, and all the sunlight gets wasted. Have your sellers open the vertical blinds so they are level. This lets the full light flood the room!

Of course, if a window has a terrible view, such as a brick wall only a few feet away, then you would want to keep the curtains closed. If there are vertical blinds on a window with a bad view, tip them slightly down, but not closed, so that light is still able to come in and flood the floor, but the potential purchaser isn't immediately struck by a horrible view.

Tip 4: Have the Stereo on All Day for All Viewings

Have every one of your sellers turn on music throughout the house as soon as they get up in the morning and keep it on all day, even if they leave. Share this wonderful secret with your sellers! Soft FM background music is best, not hard rock or "funeral music." You never know when an agent might want to bring a potential buyer to the house. Agents almost always try to set up appointments so sellers know when someone is coming. But sometimes an agent will be escorting a purchaser to another house, and as they pass by your sellers' house, the purchaser will say, "Wait a minute! Look! What about this one? I like the way this home looks outside." The agent will most likely say, "Wonderful." They'll pull up across the street, ask the purchaser to wait a minute and go to the door. Then they'll ask the sellers, "Could I show your home? Would this be a convenient time?" The sellers may not have time to turn on the stereo and the lights in the dark rooms. So, advise your sellers to keep the radio and lights turned on all day.

Tip 5: Keep the House Neat and Clean All the Time

Remind your sellers not to let the house get cluttered or dirty after you have *Staged* it with them. If they have children, ask them to be sure they pick up after themselves. You and I know that task can get tiring after you've been on the market several weeks. But tell your sellers that the day they let things slide will, without fail, be the day a potential purchaser for their home will walk through the door. That's life! Keep encouraging and complimenting your sellers as time goes on so that the property is *always Staged.*

WORK EQUALS MORE MONEY—FOR YOUR SELLERS AND YOU!

I recommend that you say, "Mr. and Mrs. Seller, you are earning yourself money by the time and energy you spend getting your home ready to sell and keeping it that way." Purchasers are very selective when it comes to finding a home of their choice. So, you and your sellers need to make the property the very best buy available on the market in comparison with all the other homes. Share this concept with your sellers.

Encourage your sellers to look at their home through the eyes of a potential buyer, as though they have never seen it before. Any time or money spent on the items I have mentioned may bring back more money in return, and almost always results in a faster sale. So tell your sellers, "You know, we are going to be making you money. And working together, we make a great team!"

Staging your listings works! I hope that the ideas and techniques in the last two chapters will help you help more sellers. The concepts work. They will work for you as they have for me and the thousands of other real estate professionals who have attended my seminars and workshops. My *Staging* video is also helping thousands of agents and offices help their sellers to properly prepare their homes for sale.

FIGURE 14-1

THE DIFFERENCE STAGING MAKES

To help you get an even better idea of the difference *Staging* can make in a home's appearance outside, here are some "before" and "after" pictures of a house before it was listed (it was For Sale by Owner) and after it was *Staged* (Figure 14-1). It doesn't even look like the same house, but it really is! What a difference *Staging* can make. It is like a miracle but is really so easy to do.

15

Ways to Ensure that Sellers Finish Preparing Their Home for Sale

In this chapter you will learn

1. The steps to take for getting the commitment from your sellers to finish preparing their home for sale.

2. How to ensure that your sellers finish preparing their home for sale.

After you have gone through the entire property with your sellers, you should have a list of things that they are going to complete and piles of things for them to put away when you leave. How do you ensure that the sellers will get everything done and put away when you are gone? This chapter is the answer to getting the list done every time by your sellers. It is indeed the icing on the cake.

THE LIST!

Once you finish going through the property with your sellers, inside and out, the sellers should know precisely what they need to do. Everything that hasn't already been fixed or added to a pile is on the list.

Never— I repeat— never just hand the list over to the sellers, then leave, and expect them to finish all the tasks while you start marketing their home. You can't be sure it will get done.

For years agents in our industry have been giving sellers lists, going back to their offices and starting all of their work to represent their sellers, but somehow the list never got done. It is time that we get a commitment from the sellers to finish all agreed-upon items. How can we really do the best possible job until they do? It takes commitments on both sides, and I don't just mean the commitment of the sellers giving us the listing on their home. I am sure you have promised the sellers many marketing commitments, and I believe one of the commitments *they* should make and uphold is to finish the list that together you agreed should and would be done. Remember, if they could not repair something about the home then I am sure you priced it accordingly. We are talking about the three C's of *Staging* and putting away the piles and getting the list done.

GETTING COMMITMENT TO FINISH LIST
AND PACK UP PILES

Getting the commitment from your sellers to complete the list of things to do should not be a problem at this point. One of the reasons I think we have had problems with this in the past is because we did not educate the sellers enough up front about the importance of preparing their home for sale. After all, if you have educated them on the importance of *Staging* from the very beginning, they should be eager to get everything completed.

Follow the few upcoming steps and you will get solid commitments from your sellers without any problems, and everything will get done.

Step 1: Be Sure They Have the List

I promise you, by the time you finish going over your sellers' property with them, you will have a nice-sized list. Many times, I'll hand a three-page list to my sellers, and I'll say with a chuckle or laugh, "Oh, I'm so proud of you. Many of my sellers have five-page lists!" They usually laugh. And I pat them on the back.

I always want to make my sellers feel good about what they are doing. "I'm so proud of you," is a phrase I highly recommend. Praise your sellers for a job well done. We all enjoy praise, and it goes a long way in building and maintaining rapport with your sellers. So, don't be afraid to pat them on the back once in a while.

Finishing that list usually does not mean they have to spend a bundle of money; rather, finishing that list will *make* them money. What it does mean is time and energy. Be sure to remind your sellers of that fact. When they are looking at a list that is going to take maybe a weekend of their time, tell them that the time and energy they spend on their home is going to earn them money.

Step 2: Have the Sellers Set a Deadline for Completing the List and Putting the Piles Away

After you have handed your sellers the list, you must get a commitment as to when the list will be done. Ask them, "Mr. and Mrs. Seller, when do you think that you can get these things done?" This is very important. If you don't ask for their commitment on a completion time, the work may never get done. It's human nature.

For years agents have been making lists of things for their sellers to do, but have not gotten a time commitment from the sellers as to when the list would be totally completed. Always ask for a specific time. Your sellers already know how important this is and most of them will dig in immediately and give their commitment for two days or even one day from now. If they begin to evade the question, gently pin them down. When you say, "Now, Mr. and Mrs. Seller, when will you be able to finish this list? When do you think you can get this done?" they may say, "Well, this is Friday. It won't be this weekend because we have to take the boy scouts camping."

In that case, say, "Well, I can understand that. But to have your home on the market and for me to start my marketing program for you, I need to know when you think you can get this list done." You've just passed the ball right back to them.

You must keep asking until you get an answer and the commitment. I have even suggested, at certain times, that sellers take off a day from work to get their $50,000 cash equity out of their home by finishing the list. I remind them, in that case, that they probably don't make $50,000 in one or two days where they work. Sometimes, they'll look at each other and say something like, "Well, let's see, we'll be home every night next week. We can get it all done in two nights' work if we really work hard and stick to it. OK, it will all be done on Wednesday and Thursday nights."

Then summarize what they have just agreed to: "Then it sounds to me like Wednesday and Thursday evenings the two of you are going to be working on the house, and you plan to get it all done then by Thursday evening. Is that correct?" If that's not right, then keep pressing for a deadline. You *must* get a deadline, and you must get it now. If you don't get it now, you probably never will. Getting the deadline from your sellers is extremely crucial. Get the day and time of day— afternoon, morning, or evening.

Step 3: Tell Your Sellers You Will Call Them the Night of Their Deadline

When you have a firm commitment from your sellers to finish the list, tell them that you will be calling them the night of the deadline. But it is crucial that you tell them now what you will be telling them then!

For example, you can say something like, "Mr. and Mrs. Seller, I am so pleased that you will have everything finished by Thursday evening, and I will be calling you then to say 'Mr. and Mrs. Seller, this is Barb. Did you get the list done? Did you get it all done?' And if you answer, 'Oh, Barb we worked so hard and we got it all done. The house looks absolutely great. Wait until you see it.' Then I will tell you Thursday evening: 'Oh, I'm so proud of you. Since you got the whole list done, I can bring my office over on tour next Monday. I can turn in your first ad because you got the whole list done. I can hold open house on Sunday, make and distribute your first flyer, and start all my marketing efforts, and they will be effective because you got your whole list done.'"

"But, Mr. and Mrs. Seller, if when I call you on Thursday evening you say, 'Oh, Barb we only got our list half done. We had unexpected company, and we just couldn't get it done.' Then I'll have to say, 'Mr. and Mrs. Seller, I can't really bring my office over on tour Monday because you didn't get your list done. I can't turn in your first ad because you didn't get your list done. I can't hold open house on Sunday, or make and distribute your first flyer. I can't start to show the buyers through your home. In other words, I cannot effectively start all my marketing on your behalf because if I did, the buyers coming through will remember what they see, not the way it's going to be. I can't start my part and make it effective until you get your part done.'" If you tell them this now it will make it so much easier to tell them again later if you need to.

I feel very strongly about this! Think about how our industry has worked for years. For years, we, as agents, have given sellers lists that somehow never quite got done. Do you know why? I'll tell you why. It is because we have given sellers lists and then gone back to our offices and started all of our marketing efforts before the sellers ever finished their lists. No wonder they never finished. We took away all of their motivation. We did this by starting our marketing before they finished their part. Don't misunderstand me, never hold back listings from the multiple. In some areas you could lose your license if you were to do that. Turn in the listing. But do not start your marketing efforts until the sellers finish their list. Make it a firm professional policy. It works!

For years I have explained to sellers that for them to get the most amount of their equity from all my marketing efforts, they must finish their part first. Sellers easily understand why, when you explain that buyers and agents only know what they see, not the way it's going to be. That way everyone's effort can be as effective as possible. If you start bringing agents and potential purchasers through the house before the sellers have packed everything away, painted what needs to be painted, or cleaned up the outside of the house, then you are not maximizing your marketing efforts. It does not make sense for you to start your marketing program, which is the best I know of, until your sellers' house is ready to go on the market.

So ask for that commitment, and settle for nothing less than a firm answer. Then, be sure your sellers follow through on their commitment, which brings me to the next step of getting a commitment from your sellers.

Step 4: Start Your Marketing Only after the Sellers Have Finished Everything on the List

Do not start your marketing program on Monday just because Sally and John told you they would finish the list by Sunday evening. You must keep your word and do what you told them. Give them a call and make sure they were able to finish everything. When you call, or better yet stop by, people don't lie. They know you will be seeing it for yourself on the commitment day. Once in a great while it takes longer than they expected. Or maybe something prevented them from finishing the list. Whatever the reason, don't start your marketing until the house is ready.

This is why from the very beginning you make sure all your sellers realize *Staging* their property correctly and thoroughly is in their best interest. Educate them that the number one thought here is to sell their home by maximizing all your efforts. You have to be working together for that same purpose. I have never yet had a seller who did not finish what we had agreed needed to be done. I believe this is because I took the time to educate my sellers as to how important *Staging* is. The other element here is motivation. Show me a seller who wants to sell, and I'll show you someone who will *Stage* his or her home. If you ever have sellers who do not finish the list you both agreed on, then I would seriously question their motivation. Do they want to sell or don't they? Preparing their home for sale is the best and fastest way I know to get their money.

Let your sellers know that, if they have finished all their work, you can begin yours. Give them an incentive for finishing the work. Also, tell them that nothing can happen if they have not finished the list. For example, let's say you called, and they said, "Oh, we didn't get the list done. We finished most of it, but we didn't get to Johnny's room, and we didn't have time to move all the lumber from the back yard." Make sure they understand that even if it is just one item, you can't start doing any of your marketing. You can say something like, "You see, Mr. and Mrs. Seller, if I held your house open and started showing your home, the agents and purchasers would remember what they see, not the way your house will look when all the things on your list have been finished." Explain to them again that your marketing is much less effective if they have not adequately prepared the property for sale. Get a commitment from them as to when they will complete their list and then repeat the process of steps 3 and 4. Remain firm, but also be very positive. They will finish their list without delay, and you can get on with the marketing.

> **Staging homes makes great sense for everyone in every market!**

Sometimes agents I meet in my seminar programs say to me, "Three months after I listed the property, my sellers still hadn't cleaned up the debris around the house. They still hadn't painted the kids' bedrooms. They never did get around to fixing the leaky shower." I ask them, "Did you get a commitment from the sellers to repair all those things before you started your marketing?" The answer from that agent always comes back to me, "No, I didn't."

I'll tell you the same thing I tell them: You have to get that commitment from your sellers! I will not start my marketing program with my sellers until they have completed that commitment, and they know that. If you start your marketing before they complete their part then you just took away all your leverage, and it becomes very difficult to get them to finish.

Sometimes I have had agents attend my class on *Staging* and say, "Barb, the market is hot, and to sell the house the sellers don't even need to *Stage* it. How do you feel about this?" My answer is always the same, "Can a home ever sell for too much? Tell me, would you or your sellers like to sell the home at an even higher price?" I love it because the answer is always the same, "yes!" Agents in hot markets have already proven that homes that are *Staged* can and do sell for more. So even in really active markets, sellers should *Stage* their homes because they will probably sell for more, which means more satisfied sellers, more referral business, and more commission in your pocket to take to the bank.

In slow markets homes that are *Staged* may not sell for more, but they will sell faster than the competition that is not *Staged*. In active or slow markets the following is true:

> **Buyers only know what they see,
> not the way it's going to be.**

and

> **The way we live in a home and the way we
> sell a home are two different things.**

QUALITY APPEARANCE

I believe it is crucial to our success as residential real estate agents to properly *Stage* our properties for sale. The time is long overdue for us to represent merchandise only when it is at its best. Your name is hanging on the sign in the front yard. Your image with other agents and the public is based on the quality appearance of properties you list. Accept the challenge to do your best for your sellers and take the steps to do it now. You will be amazed at what can happen— for your sellers and for your career!

16

Organization and Success

In this chapter you will learn

1. How to organize your three workstations.
2. How to get the most from your time.

As you begin to use what you have learned by reading this book, you will begin to obtain more and more listings, so to survive success you must be organized.

SUCCESS BY GETTING YOUR ACT TOGETHER!

Using what I have shared with you in this book, you now know how to put together what I believe is the strongest Exclusive Marketing Program and the most effective listing presentation available in the industry today. Thousands and thousands of real estate agents throughout the country are using this program, and say it is the most practical, proven program to come along in years. It makes such good sense. I know with the information supplied in this book, you can become as successful as you would like to be. It is only a matter of getting started. Even if I ended this book on this page, you could start making more money right now. But I want to give you more. I want to share with you a few tips on getting the best results from your work.

Organize in Self-Defense

If you want a smooth journey to success, get organized. The best defense is definitely a good offense! Now, you may be saying to yourself, "These stacks of paper on my desk only look like a mess. Actually I know where everything is." But, I caution you, if you follow the program I have outlined for you, those piles on your desk are going to grow into monsters, which will eat you alive because you are now going to have more business than ever before. The number of properties you list will increase; therefore, so will your paperwork and the demands on your time. You will need to be organized just so your greater success doesn't overwhelm you!

THREE AREAS TO ORGANIZE

You may not realize it, but you have three offices. If you want to be poised for action— and success— you need to have each one of these "offices" organized in such a way that you can conduct business no matter where you are.

Area 1: Your Desk at the Office

Obviously, you have everything you need at your company's office. The forms, the supplies, and other day-to-day items such as paper clips, staplers, and so forth, are close at hand in a supply closet or storage area, right? So, you shouldn't have to do too much improving in this area. But what is the condition of your desk? Do you have a few copies of all the forms you use in a desk drawer? Do you have at your fingertips more than one pen that writes? Just think how much simpler life would be if you had everything you needed right there with you. No more rushing around to find supplies when someone comes into your office to make an offer on one of your listings. No more rummaging around for a form when you are rushing out the door! So, organize your desk drawers, and be sure you have everything you could possibly need for business right there with you.

One good way to control the clutter on your desk top is to use file baskets. With "In," "Out," and "Do It Now!" baskets, you can save your desk from sinking in a sea of paper and yourself from the danger of losing important documents. Touch each paper only once! I know that can be hard, but be tough on yourself. The day I started acting like every paper I picked up was stuck to my fingers like glue until I did something with it, I really started to save time and change my work habits. Have you ever noticed how often you pick up the same piece of paper without doing something in the form of action to get that piece of paper put away or thrown away once and for all? Work hard to touch each paper only once. The time and energy you save by keeping your desk organized can be spent obtaining more listings and earning more money!

Area 2: Your Desk at Home

The same rules for your office desk apply to your desk at home. You want to be able to do the same work and answer the same calls at home as you can at your office. In real estate, there is no such time as "after hours".

The main difference between your desk at home and the one at the office is that you need to have some extra supplies at home. You can't just run to the supply closet if you need a form when someone calls. Now, I am not suggesting you wipe out your company's supplies, but taking a few extra copies of each form is not going to hurt your company. It will help the company when you use those forms to write up an agreement or fill out a change order to drop a price. It will help you, and it helps the company by enabling you to perform a particular service quickly because you had the items you needed. So, keep your desk at home neat and well stocked.

Incidentally, I found having a desk at home was a big help. Many times interruptions happen too easily at the office, and you may end up wasting too much time just talking to others in your office. Having an extra desk at home can help you make more phone calls without as many interruptions. I used to say to my managers, "Don't look for me in the office too much, because if I'm in here I'm not making money. I need to be out where the buyers and sellers are, or at certain times making calls from home where I can't be interrupted." It worked. I went in the office only when I needed to.

This also helped me when my daughter was young. In this way I could be with her and still make all of my phone calls and prepare paperwork that needed to be done. I would be remiss if I didn't share this fact with those of you who have children. There were even a few times, and I kept it to only a few, when I actually had to take her with me. She and I talked about how she should act in that situation, and how she was helping Mom earn money for the family so that we could do things, such as trips, together. When push came to shove I did it, and it worked.

Area 3: Last, but Certainly not Least—Your Car

If you are like me, you spend at least as much (if not more) time in your car as you do at your office or home. So, your car needs to be organized. Also, these days you can make or receive calls in your car and save a lot of time doing just that. Invest in a car phone. I find it is just like a dishwasher; once you have one you can't live without it. I have saved many a sale from my car using that phone when a problem came up before the sale closed. It really is invaluable! And that is true for fax machines and computers as well.

Now, I have a simple system for the car that works beautifully. Try it if you don't already have one of your own. With what I call my "trunk and two-box system," you can turn your car into an office on wheels! This system enables you to go anywhere and still be able to function as well as if you were at the office— maybe even better!

TWO-BOX SYSTEM

Box 1:

Have one box in the trunk of your car that holds a few copies of every form you could possibly need. In other words, have copies of all the forms you would use in the office. I'm talking about purchase and sale agreement forms, change-order forms, rent-back forms, addendums, any kind of form that you need in your day-to-day real estate career. Have them with you so if you go to see your sellers, and all of a sudden they decide to change something, you don't need to go back to the office to get a form to make the change. You have the appropriate form with you at all times!

Of course, you can carry some of these forms in your briefcase. But if you run out of them, you can just go out to your car to get more forms, instead of going back to the office. Get into the habit of restocking the supplies in your car as soon you notice you are running low. Always have the forms with you.

In your car keep a box full of various note pads, envelopes, company stationery, and other writing supplies. You never know when you are going to be kept waiting— maybe you have to use ferries in your area, or you might be stuck on the freeway, or detained at a railroad crossing. If you have these supplies with you, you can write a letter to someone whenever you are delayed. It is a great way to keep thank you notes going out every day, and to stay in touch with prospects and other agents!

Box 2:

In the second box be sure to always have such things as a staple gun and staples, nails, "SOLD" signs, hammers, screwdrivers, signs, arrows, toilet paper, and don't forget the dog biscuits! You now have things in your trunk that can help you do a better job. Great— more power to you! Anything and everything you think

you are going to need at one time or another should be in your
car, either in the back seat or in the trunk.

ORGANIZATION IS THE NAME OF THE GAME

I hope you are a person who is usually organized, but if you are
not, you will need to be, in real estate. Don't procrastinate! If
you keep these three areas—your office, desk, and car—organized, you should always have what you need when you need
it. Being prepared and organized can make the difference between listing one home in a week, or listing a half-dozen. And,
remember to keep your *Career Books* and *Marketing Portfolio* in
your back seat, so you have them as you need them!

TIME MANAGEMENT

Being organized also means getting the most from the time
you have. We all have the same amount of time—twenty-four
hours every day. But have you ever noticed how some people
seem to get so much more done in that time than others? Well,
the secret of effective time management is really no secret—it
is a matter of getting your entire career organized, not just
your car and desks. I want to share with you a few tips that,
if you follow them, are guaranteed to help you use your time
more effectively.

Tip 1: Schedule Your Time

That doesn't sound too complicated, does it? Putting yourself on a schedule doesn't mean giving up personal freedom. In
reality, it gives you freedom. When you are organized, which
includes having a schedule of all the things you need to do each
day, you will be amazed at how much time you can save. And
the time you save is yours. You will have more time for presentations, which means more listings. You will have more time for
marketing, which means more sales!

So, plan and schedule your days. And schedule time off for
yourself. It may be the only way you'll get it.

If you have five houses to check out tomorrow, write yourself a schedule of what houses you are going to see, when you are going to see them, and what you will do on each visit. You will find you can keep yourself better organized when you know what you are going to be doing most of the day and in what order. Start scheduling your activities, including nonbusiness activities. If you are having lunch with your mother, include that in your schedule. Then stick to the schedule unless something really important comes up. I always ask myself every day what is the most productive thing I can do today to bring about a listing or a sale and then I do it.

Tip 2: Build in Flexibility

Don't put yourself on such a strict schedule, though, that if an appointment is canceled you are robbed of two productive hours. Be prepared for delays and changes. This goes back to my advice about keeping company stationery and notepads in your car. Use spare time to review an upcoming presentation or to contact prospects. Don't just spend time— invest it!

Tip 3: Use Travel Time to Your Advantage

Why not put that time to work for you? As I said before, most real estate agents practically live in their cars. If you are on a trip between cities, listen to an educational cassette or use the time to brainstorm for an upcoming marketing program or presentation. Practice what you want to say out loud. No one can hear you, and I found if I practiced out loud in my car on the way to appointments, I had a much higher rate of success. Much of the program you have read in this book on listing residential real estate I thought of and practiced out loud, day after day, year after year, as I worked with the hundreds of sellers for whom I listed and sold properties. They say practice makes perfect, and I truly believe it does.

Schedule appointments in the same areas closer together when you can. If you have to see three houses that are stretched out across your area, try to arrange the visits so you can cover them all in a line without backtracking.

Tip 4: Keep a Daily "To-Do" and "To-Call" List

Keep a list of all those things you must do—and do them! This list is for the things that are easy to forget unless you write them down, such as dropping off a loan verification letter or picking up some groceries for an open house. Every night, before I go to bed, I make a "to-do" and a "to-call" list for the next day. If you really get yourself into this habit, you will find it invaluable. I also find if I dump things on my mind out onto the list before I go to bed, I do not worry about them nearly as much. You get more and better sleep that way. Try it; it works. Then the next morning you are all set. Pick up your piece of paper, review it, and get going.

Tip 5: Conquer Bad Habits that Waste Time

Work to eliminate these bad habits that can devour your precious time.

- Habitually leaving your home or office a few minutes late.
- Turning business calls into "social" visits. It's all right to build rapport, but don't forget that you are there for business.
- Spending too much time over lunch with a friend or on other nonbusiness matters.
- Not disciplining yourself to get your work done on time.
- Spending too much time socializing with associates in your office.

If any of these are bad habits for you, when you overcome these you will be amazed at how much more time you really will have.

Tip 6: Stop Procrastinating—Do It Now

We all do it. We wait until tomorrow or the next day to do what should have been done today or yesterday. All you have to do is make up your mind to do things as they come up. If you have an ad to deliver to your local newspaper for the Sunday edition, then get to it. If you need to pick up your *Career Book* from a For Sale by Owner, don't wait until the end of the week. Go get it today, and sell that For Sale by Owner on how you can help sell his or her house.

If you have a tough call you have to make then do it first thing in the morning. The rest of your day will be a breeze and much more fun because you dealt with the tough thing first instead of putting it off to last, or not doing it at all.

Procrastination is the biggest killer of sales. "Do it now" is the best advice I can give. No matter what it is, do it now.

GOLD MINE

You have a gold mine in your hands. And you now have the pick that is going to help you mine the gold. The gold is all around you. Remember what I said earlier: Everyone is a prospect. Sooner or later, almost everyone who owns a home is going to sell a home. In this book, I have given the best strategies and techniques I know for becoming more successful at listing residential real estate.

I have taught you my concept of the *Career Book* and how it can really bridge the credibility gap. I have outlined my Exclusive Marketing Program for you and shown you exactly how to use it, not only in your listing presentations but for actually selling homes. I have shown you how to *Stage* homes, and why it works and why it is a necessity in your marketplace. I know you are going to put the techniques and tips I have given you to use. That is why you will soon be making more money than you have ever made.

But we're not quite finished. I want to talk to you about one more thing— the greater success you are destined to find!

17

Your Journey of Success

In this chapter you will learn

1. The importance of setting goals and working toward them.
2. A brief review of what you have learned in this book.
3. Some encouraging words on "failure" and "success."

As you go on your journey of success, it really helps if you know which direction to start. One step in the right direction is to set goals for yourself and then work for those goals.

DEVELOPMENT OF A PLAN

Where are you on your journey to success? You need to know where you are going, or else you may never get there.

Can you imagine getting into your car, starting the engine, driving down your driveway without having the slightest idea of where you are going? Of course not. However, that's the way many people approach their careers. They jump into it, work very hard, and just go, go, go. But they sometimes don't make any progress. They end up running around in circles with no idea where they are headed. They have no direction; they have no specific goals.

What about you? What are your goals? Toward what are you striving? Do you have a plan for reaching those goals? Some people live by setting goals, and others are confused or afraid to try because they think they might fail. I hope you will try if you never have set goals before; it's a lot easier than you think, and it can bring you greater success than you ever dreamed possible.

STEPS FOR REACHING GOALS

I know most people have their own goals, and I would never try to tell you what yours should be. But I do believe in the power of having goals, as I have seen literally what seemed like miracles happen in my own life from setting goals. I also believe in a system or program to make goals happen. I know this system works for me and has worked for millions of others. Like everything else I have shared with you, you can adapt these strategies to your own style.

Step 1: Define Your Goals

In residential real estate, you can easily divide your goals into several manageable categories, such as:

Homes You Want to List. This includes any prospects you have already talked with and names you have seen as possible prospects, such as a For Sale by Owner. I believe everyone is a prospect, but this list should be limited to specific people who you think are hot listing candidates. You should also set a goal of how many properties you want to list on a weekly, monthly, or yearly basis.

Buyers You Want to Sell. You also have buyer prospects that you can pursue. Don't forget your past and present sellers, and ask for referrals from sellers and buyers. You should set goals based on a number of buyers you want to work with during a certain period. Then, target specific people.

Sales You Want to Close. Getting your listings sold is a primary goal, but the name of the game is, of course, getting those sales to close so that everyone can get paid. This list includes only the names of buyers and sellers for whom a sale is already in the process of closing. You may need to direct some attention to the details of the closing.

Income You Want to Earn. You can set your sights on a dollar figure that you want to earn. The key here (and with all goals) is to come up with a figure that is *realistic*— one that you will have to work and stretch a little to reach, but also one that can be achieved. It does nothing for your confidence if you set a goal that is unrealistically high, and you fail to reach it.

You can use one or all of these categories, or create your own. Remember, the only right way is the one that works for you. Once you have defined your goals and divided them into categories, I suggest that you quantitatively break them down into smaller increments so that you can actually see how you can achieve them.

For example, let's say that you set a goal of listing four homes next month. How can that be done? Well, that's only one new listing a week, a much more specific target. Then analyze how you can do it. How many listing presentations will you need to give, based on past experience, to get one listing? How many phone calls, contacts, or referrals will you need to work to generate each listing presentation? If you work backward in this manner you can even set goals for your daily work to achieve your weekly, monthly, or yearly goals.

Always divide your clients and goals into categories. They are much easier to manage that way. You won't feel overwhelmed, and you will be much better organized.

Step 2: Commit Your Goals to Writing

Write all of your goals down on paper. Every expert in the field suggests you do that because it forces you to make more of a commitment than if you just think about something you'd like to achieve. Let's say you have met four new families, and you want to list them all. Don't just think about those families, write down their names. Get yourself a notebook, and write down their names monthly under a heading that reads, "I am listing these homes." Notice the list does not say, "I want to list these homes." It says "I am listing these homes." If you don't get the listing the first day it is on the list, write it under that heading again the next day.

Defining your goals in black and white gives them dimension and can make them more real for you. This works miracles. Written goals give you something concrete to work toward. Written goals happen!

When I started writing down my goals, as I have just explained, the most wonderful things did begin to happen— and those of you who have tried this know what I am talking about— all of a sudden I was listing the homes I had written under that heading. The mind does the work it needs to do to achieve the goals we have expressed on paper. And that is the most exciting thing about setting goals and the capabilities of our human mind. More on that later!

Step 3: Visualize the Goal as Reality in Your Mind

After you have defined your goals and added them to your written list, visualize the goals as reality. For example, I have written down the sales that are already in escrow that I am going to close. If I have the sale on paper, whether I was the listing agent or the selling agent, there is no reason in my mind why the sale shouldn't close. If I know I have done my work— my marketing, qualifying, and follow-up— then there is no reason that sale shouldn't close. So I will actually visualize myself with the sellers signing the closing documents. Visualization works.

Many different doctors, educators, and philosophers have written about this concept. A short explanation of this phenomenon is that the brain cannot differentiate between stimuli from the conscious mind and those from the subconscious mind. The act of visualizing your goals and actually putting them down on paper starts to create a "reality" in the brain that this thought (goal) is real. The brain will then start to find ways to make the thought actually come to reality. If you think this all sounds too good to be true, I hope you will trust me that it really is true. If you would like to know more, I suggest you read one of the many books available on this subject. The more you see your goals happening in your own mind, the more your brain will seek a way to make it happen in real life.

So define your goals. Then write them down. Visualize the end result you want, and it will come to life right in front of you. Write down the people you want to help. Write down the sales you have in escrow. Write down the number of new listings you want next month. Believe in your goals. Believe you are going to list those four families. Believe you are going to find the perfect home for the purchaser. Believe and visualize that you are going to close the sale. Believe, and you will make it happen! This is because anything that your mind can conceive and you believe, you can achieve.

I hope that you will make goal-setting a permanent part of your personal and professional life. Millions of people have found that working toward goals gives them structure, confidence, success, and gives them the ability to get what they want out of their lives and careers.

COURAGE TO TRY!

In this book I have discussed and introduced practical ideas and techniques that work. Through my own years as a real estate broker and in the past five years as a national speaker and trainer, wherever I go, people say to me, "Barb, I never thought about or heard about a *Career Book* before. I am so glad you shared that idea. You have changed the course of real estate and the ways in which we, as agents, can let our sellers know who we are and what we have done in the business for others. I am listing more homes using the *Career Book* than I ever have before. I also never knew how a *Marketing Portfolio* could help me, and I put it together and now I've got a listing presentation that is so powerful, I get every listing I want. It works like dynamite!

"And, you have changed the way property comes on the market with your *Staging* techniques. You are cleaning up America, and we are all benefiting from it. Those of us using your ideas are taking them to the bank!"

In fact this message was waiting for me on my answering machine one day as I returned to my office late in the evening: "Hi, Barb! This is Mary, and I attended your seminar last week. I decided to really follow through and put together a *Career Book* and a *Marketing Portfolio*. I just thought you would want to know I used them yesterday and last night. I couldn't believe it. Your ideas, tools, and program worked like a miracle. The sellers said it was the most professional presentation they had ever seen, and I got the listing. Thank you so much!"

So, my advice to you is to follow through with what you have learned in this book. Keep an open mind, try to use the ideas I have shared with you. Adapt what you have learned to your own style and personality, and take them to the bank!

ONE LAST LOOK

To end our time together I would like to take you through a quick review which I hope will tie everything together for you and also give you a place you can go to read, remember, and review my main concepts on listing with control any time you want. Repetition is the mother of learning, so please review this or any other part of this book often. This is the key to changing any behavior and learning new concepts. If you do review, you will learn, grow, change the way you do things, and be more successful. This is true of your career in real estate as well as any new change you want to undertake in your life.

Let Me Tell You How I Work

Be sure you spend time during your first contact with any seller to explain an overview of the services you provide. Set yourself apart from other agents right away. Sellers won't understand or appreciate you or your Exclusive Marketing Program if you don't explain it to them. When you go to another professional for help or advice, you don't know how that person works unless he or she tells you. You won't go wrong, I promise you, if you tell them the following up front: "Let me tell you how I work, Mr. and Mrs. Seller. Here is what I am going to be doing for you." Not only will you take care of objections before they come up, but most people appreciate being told the ways you can serve them. So, sell yourself by telling people up front how you work.

Take Time to Educate the Sellers—They Deserve It

> **Remember, Education = Control.**

Spend at least two visits with your prospective sellers. The time is worth it. Tell sellers, "Mr. and Mrs. Seller, I believe in giving you a lot of service. I am going to spend time with you in the listing of your home, so that you will fully understand all that I will do for you."

Put Together a *Career Book* to Help Sell You

Be proud of who you are. Remember there is much more to you than meets the eye. If *you* don't sell you, then who will? No one, that's who. People don't know what you don't tell them, and that is true about how special you are as well. The beautiful thing is that your *Career Book* will do the talking for you, so you don't have to worry about bragging.

The *Career Book* will show off your professional side so that sellers will have more confidence and trust in you. It will show off your personal side too, so that you can develop common ground with your sellers, a real hidden key to getting more business. Put one together, and do it now. Also, when you leave it with clients and customers, you are "living" in the property, and you have a perfectly logical reason to go back because you have to pick up your book.

Remember the Three Steps of Great Service

Step 1. Meet the sellers and see their property. Be sure you have the sellers show you their property, as no one knows the home like they do. Work to build rapport and then leave your *Career Book*, which details your real estate experience and how your expertise will help them. Tell them, "I'd really appreciate your taking the time to look at my *Career Book*. It will help you get to know me better. I think you'll enjoy it!" Review your "Let me tell you how I work" plan with them so they fully understand all of your great service and what's going to happen next. Then just set the appointment to return for your listing presentation (Detailed Report).

Step 2. Present your Detailed Report to your future sellers. The Detailed Report is in two parts: First, your marketing ("here's what I'm going to do to sell your property"), and second, pricing ("this is a price range in which I think your property should be listed in today's market").

During your marketing presentation be sure to have a written Exclusive Marketing Program that lists all of the marketing you will do for the sale of their home and a *Marketing Portfolio* to show off all your marketing techniques. This visual aid will give you a truly professional and powerful listing presentation that will set you apart from most other agents. Explain to them that you will show them what you plan to do to market their home, before they authorize a listing agreement with you. They deserve to know all of the marketing you are going to do ahead of time. Spend plenty of time to educate your sellers fully on all the techniques you will use to market their home.

For pricing I recommend that you first spend time educating your sellers on the market conditions that will affect them. Show them solds, expireds, and the competition. Again, take time to educate them during your Comparative Market Analysis so they will respect and accept your professional analysis of where they fit in today's market in price and terms.

At the end of your Detailed Report, which is a real information-sharing time for them, zero in on a realistic and competitive list price using my pricing triangle. It works.

Step 3. First, complete the actual paperwork for listing of the sellers' property. Remember to take enough time to be thorough and accurate with your listing agreement. It's important.

Then, "with their permission," go through their home with them, room by room, to make recommendations about things to do and things to put away to prepare their home for sale. *Staging* works, so don't shy away from it. If you are uncomfortable talking to sellers about *Staging* you can use my video to explain it for you. It will help you help your sellers sell their property faster in a slow market, and in a hot market *Staging* will help the sellers obtain a higher selling price.

USE ALL OF THE MARKETING TECHNIQUES

These marketing techniques work. They sell listings, and they sell you! Sure, you have to work. But the rewards are worth it. If you follow my marketing plan, you can watch your sales volume— and your income— grow!

Try doing all the things that I've shared in this book, because I know they will work for you. Build and use a *Career Book*. Try the three steps. Put together a *Marketing Portfolio*. Tell your prospects how you work and educate them about how you list and sell homes. Last, but definitely not least, *Stage* your listings. You won't be disappointed!

SUCCESS!

I sincerely hope reading this book has been a valuable experience for you. You are so special. There has never been anyone quite like you. You can adapt what you have learned to your own style and situation. You can list residential real estate successfully!

I truly believe there are no real failures, only experiences! You can't fail— you only experience! The only failure is just giving up.

So learn from your experiences. Learn and grow. Step out and step up! I challenge you to try something new, something that stretches you as a person. Take a risk, even if it's just a small one to start with, and you will be taking a step of growth. When you think about it, everything in life is really a risk— some are just more scary than others. But the greater the risk, the higher the gain. Some people coast; they do things the same old way, never really changing or trying new ideas. You know what? They usually coast downhill.

Enjoy your journey. Keep at this adventure called life. Success is the journey itself, not just an end. As a real estate agent, an educator, a speaker, an author, and now, I hope, your new friend, I want to thank you for this opportunity to share with you what I have learned. Step out and apply what you have learned. Try something new and grow! Do it, and do it now! I wish you happiness. I wish you love. And I wish you success!

Appendix

Pages 212–229 contain copies of forms and information which you may find helpful as you list and sell residential real estate. These pages can be enlarged and copied for use in your own career. Include them in your *Career Book* or *Marketing Portfolio,* or wherever you will find them most useful.

Barb's Favorite Sayings Words That Work

Pre-Listing Phrases

"Should we decide that we will be working together . . ."

"I'd really appreciate you taking the time to look at my Career Book.® There are ideas in it to help you sell your home and lots of ideas about who I am and what I've done in Real Estate. It will help you get to know me better without me sitting here bragging about myself. I think you'll enjoy it!"

"You are hiring me to perform a service for you."

"Ads don't sell houses — agents do. Ads make the phone ring for the company and make the seller feel good!"

"If I didn't know of your earnest money presentation and wasn't there when it was presented, it would be like you hired an attorney and he sent you to court alone."

"Just like the product on the shelf at the store, the purchaser of today buys the best available product, at the best price, in the best wrapper, to meet his/her needs."

Getting the House Ready to Sell

"If we can't see it we can't sell it!"

"Start packing because with me working as your agent, you will be moving."

"Would you consider selling a car without touching up the chips, washing/waxing it, vacuuming it for each showing and fixing any problems?" (wait for answer) "Well, do you know that many Sellers on the market have not done that with their own homes. They haven't gotten them ready to sell."

"I'm so proud of you . . ."

"The way we live in a home and the way we sell it are two different things."

"You are earning yourself money by the time and energy you spend getting your home ready to sell."

"By preparing your home for sale we will be so much farther ahead of our competition."

"Just like the product on the shelf at the store, the purchaser of today buys the best available product, at the best price, in the best wrapper, to meet his needs."

1

Pricing and Selling Their Home

"This is not the market to come on the market and just 'see' what happens."

"If we are too high in our price, the other agents won't show us, but if we are being shown and are not getting earnest moneys then the buyers think we are overpriced compared to the competition they are seeing!"

"What do you think would happen if we overpriced your home?"

"The average selling time in this market has been between the 3rd and 6th months."

"Location, condition, price and terms — these are the 4 main factors that sell homes, and of these price is the most influential — based on the other 3."

"The best time to sell a home is in the first 4 weeks!"

"When homes are listed on the market some are always used to sell others — I don't want us to be the usee — we can be the user — but not the usee."

"Most qualified buyers are working with agents."

Getting the Listing for Six Months or Longer

"The average selling time in this market has been between the 3rd and 6th months."

"As a business woman (man) it doesn't make sense for me to list a property for 3 months based on the above fact."

"As a team working together we ask certain things of each other. The commitment I ask of you is a 6 month listing agreement because of the extra work I will do for you (beyond the average agent) and the average length of selling time."

"There is no listing agreement that can't be broken. I would not want to represent someone who didn't want me to."

Use These Phrases in Everything You Do

"With your permission . . ."

"Working together as a team we can . . ."

"Trust me."

"You may not always want to hear the facts I have to share with you, but I will always give you my honest professional opinion."

"People sometimes go to the doctor for his diagnosis and then throw away or don't fill the prescription. I will always give you my honest professional opinion and it is up to you to accept or follow my recommendations."

Barb's Favorite Stories Words That Work

Where Are The Buyers?
and
The Top Agent Story

Question: *"Where are the Purchasers of Today?"*

Answer: "Most qualified buyers are working with agents!"

Question: *"Which agents?"*

Answer: "The hard working full time agents in our area!"

Question: *"Well, who are they?"*

Answer: "I decided to find out!"
So . . . I got on the phone and called every major broker in town and asked, "Who are the top three agents in your office?" They gave me their names immediately and I compiled a list of the top agents in our area. My idea was to simply drive them crazy (in a nice way) with my listings so that hopefully they would show them first because they:
#1 - Look good!
#2 - They all priced right! and . . .
#3 - My sales close!
It worked and this has helped me sell more of my listings than any other way."
This list has now grown to the top _____ agents in our area!

1/3 Market Story

During my career in Real Estate I have always felt you could divide the number of homes on the market for sale into thirds. (This is continually born out by statistics available through the Multiple Listing Association.)

If I were to draw a line on this paper, to represent the market, and divide it into thirds we would see the market fall into the following categories:

Never Sell	?	Yes!

i

© 1986 Barb Schwarz

Explanations:

Never Sell

This third will never sell! All of the "ingredients of a sale" are out of balance because the property is in a poor location, and/or the condition is bad, and/or they are grossly overpriced with no terms available, other than cash out. Until they change one or more of the "ingredients of a sale," so that they are in balance, they will never sell!

?

This third of the market is a real question-mark! These are the sellers who insist, "We could get lucky," when discussing the pricing of their home. The "ingredients of a sale" are out of balance in one way or another, but not quite as dramatically as with the "Never Sell" group. In other words, they may have great condition, or be in a super location, but still be overpriced in comparison to what the market will bear.

Yes!

This group is hot! The homes in this third of the market are priced to sell! They are in super condition, with great locations **and** they are priced at or even below what the other homes (the other 2/3 of the market) are listed at. This is what it takes to sell in today's market and the closer we are to this 1/3 of the market the **quicker** we will sell!

The Apple Story

Purchasers of today are very selective (picky, if you will) about finding the home of their choice. Because there are so many homes on the market for sale today it reminds me of going to the store to buy an apple.

You see if there are three apples for sale at the store you would probably pick up each one, look it over and select one out of the three apples to buy. And this is just what the purchasers of yesterday's Real Estate Markets used to do — buy one home after looking at very few — even as few as three.

But **today's** market is **different!** We don't have three or just a few homes for sale. On the contrary, we have an **over-abundance** of homes for sale! So, when that purchaser goes to market he/she not only looks at one or two or three homes, but **many many** homes . . . sometimes as many as 100 homes before deciding upon one home to purchase. This then is just like when we go to the store to buy an apple and there are not just three apples **but** hundreds of apples. Guess what we do? We pick up one here, look it over, and put it down and pick up one over there, look it over, and put it down, and this goes on and on until we find **just** the right one — **the perfect apple** — out of all the other apples for sale. Just so then today's purchasers in this market purchase homes the way they buy apples — only after looking many of them over. We then, working together as agent and seller, need to make your property (our listing) the very best apple (buy) available on the market today in comparison to all the others for sale.

2

Tips for Selling

"GET READY TO MOVE – START PACKING"

WHEN I LIST YOUR HOME, WE WILL GO THROUGH THE HOUSE TOGETHER.
Meanwhile, here are some of my tips for you to think about. In doing this, we will be
ahead of most of the sellers (our competition) already on the market in the way your
home shows . . .

INSIDE:

1. Clear all unnecessary objects from furniture throughout the house. Keep decorative
objects on the furniture restricted to groups of 1, 3, or 5 items.

2. Clear all unnecessary objects from the kitchen countertops. If it hasn't been used for
three months, put it away! Clear refrigerator fronts of messages, pictures, etc. (A
sparse kitchen helps the buyer mentally move *their own* things into *your* kitchen.)

3. In the bathroom, remove any unnecessary items from countertops, tubs, shower stalls
and commode tops. Keep only your most needed cosmetics, brushes, perfumes, etc.,
in one small *group* on the counter. Coordinate towels to one or two colors *only*.

4. Rearrange or remove some of the furniture if necessary. As owners, many times we
have too much furniture in a room. This is wonderful for our own personal enjoy-
ment, but when it comes to selling, we need to thin out as much as possible to make
rooms appear larger.

5. Take down, or rearrange certain pictures or objects on walls. Patch and paint if
necessary.

6. Review the house inside room by room, *and*:
a) Paint any room needing paint.
b) Clean carpets or drapes that need it.
c) Clean windows.

1

7. Make sure the closets and garage are not "too full." Rent a storage unit if necessary.

8. Leave on certain lights during the day. (I'll show you which ones). During "showings" turn on *all* lights and lamps.

9. Have stereo FM on during the day for *all* viewings.

10. Key Box — #1 Importance: "IF WE DON'T HAVE IT, THEY WON'T SHOW US!"

OUTSIDE:

1. Go around the perimeter of the house and move all garbage cans, discarded wood scraps, extra building materials, etc., into the garage.

2. Check gutters and/or roof for dry rot. Make sure they are swept and cleaned.

3. Look at all plants ... prune bushes and trees. Keep plants from blocking windows. "YOU CAN'T SELL A HOUSE IF YOU CAN'T SEE IT." Plants are like children—they grow so fast!!

4. Weed and then bark all planting areas. Keep lawn freshly cut and fertilized. Remove any dead plants or shrubs.

5. Clear patios or decks of all small items, such as small planters, flower pots, charcoal, barbecues, toys, etc. (Put them in garage.)

6. Check paint condition of the house—especially on the front door and trim. "CURB APPEAL REALLY WORKS!"

IN GENERAL:
Try to look at your house "THROUGH THE BUYER'S EYES" as though you've never seen it or been there before. Any time or money spent on these items will bring you back more money in return, and hopefully a faster sale. "WE ARE MAKING YOU MONEY!"

"WORKING TOGETHER, we make a Great Team!"

2

Recipe For A Sale

There are 5 main ingredients that make up the sale of your home:

1. LOCATION: We usually cannot move a home! To coin the favorite phrase of appraisers: "Location, Location, Location." The *pricing* of your property must reflect its location.

2. CONDITION: The upkeep and presentation of your property is *crucial* to obtain the highest value for your home in any given market at any given time. The *pricing* of your property must reflect its condition.

3. PRICE: *Price* is the *number one* factor in the sale of a home. A property is really only worth what one person is willing to pay another to gain ownership of it. *Price* must be in direct relationship to the other 4 ingredients and it is the most important of all!

4. TERMS: The more terms available on your property the more potential purchasers you reach. The pricing of your property must reflect the kinds of terms available to purchase it.

5. THE MARKET: i.e. Interest Rates, Competition, and the Economy all make up and influence the state of the Market when you sell your home. The pricing of your property must reflect the current status of the Market.

When all of the above ingredients are in agreement . . . we have a sale! If just one of them is out of line it will take a longer time to sell, and . . . the more ingredients there are out of line . . . the longer it will take before the sale of your home takes place.

CLOSING A REAL ESTATE TRANSACTION
STEPS TO CLOSE A SALE
(After a purchase and sale agreement is finalized by both buyer and seller)

(I)   Deposit earnest money in a trust account.

(II)   Buyer makes loan application at financial institution of choice if applicable.

Financial institution then performs the following:

1. Orders appraisal of property from certified appraisal company.
2. Processes credit report for the purchaser.
3. Verifies purchaser's employment.
4. Verifies purchaser's bank accounts or other monies necessary to close.
5. Orders any required inspections and oversees any necessary repairs.
6. Oversees that all conditions of the purchase and sale agreement are met before closing.
7. Consolidates all of the above into a loan package that is presented to the loan committee for final approval.
8. When final lender approval is completed all necessary information is forwarded to the designated closing agency.

(III)   Select a closing agency to coordinate the closing of the sale.

The closing agency then performs the following:

1. Orders preliminary title report.
2. Oversees and coordinates solution of any problems revealed in the preliminary title report.
3. File documents to clear title of all liens, encumbrances, judgments, clouds on title, or easement questions.
4. Orders title insurance policy.
5. Verifies that all work orders are completed and reinspected if necessary.
6. Prorates any rents, taxes, or utilities to the date of closing.
7. Prepares all documents and closing papers for buyer and seller to sign.
8. Arranges for both parties to sign closing documents.
9. Files all documents with the local government to close the sale.
10. Upon closing, disburses funds per the closing instructions.

As your professional real estate agent I will be working hard on an ongoing basis to ensure that all of these steps take place in a timely manner as we work together towards a closed sale.

Pricing Your Home

There are _____ homes for sale in your area

priced between _____ and _____

The total number of homes on the market is _____

We Cannot Control:
Location
The Market, i.e.
   Interest Rates
   Competition
   Economy

We Can Control:
Condition
Price
Terms

 $ _____ up ↑

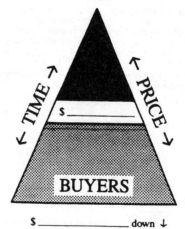

$ _____ down ↓

Homes For Sale On The Market

MY EXCLUSIVE
MARKETING PROGRAM
FOR
THE SALE OF YOUR HOME

MY LISTING PROCESS

1. PREPARE A COMPARATIVE MARKET ANALYSIS OF YOUR HOME.
2. DETERMINE THE BEST POSSIBLE LIST PRICE FOR YOUR HOME IN TODAY'S MARKET.
3. COMPLETE AND REVIEW THE LISTING AGREEMENT WITH YOU.
4. **PREPARE YOUR HOME FOR SALE.** SPEND AS MUCH TIME AS NEEDED TO GO OVER THE ENTIRE PROPERTY WITH YOU, BOTH INSIDE AND OUTSIDE. I WILL MAKE A LIST, WITH YOU, OF SUGGESTIONS AND RECOMMENDATIONS ABOUT YOUR HOME SO IT WILL SHOW AT ITS VERY BEST DURING ITS TIME ON THE MARKET.
5. INSTALL A KEY BOX AND OUR EXCLUSIVE FOR SALE SIGN.
6. CREATE A PROFESSIONAL INFORMATION SHEET HIGHLIGHTING THE KEY SELLING POINTS OF YOUR HOME FOR PROSPECTIVE PURCHASERS.
7. PREPARE YOUR INDIVIDUAL MARKETING BOOKLET TO BE LEFT IN YOUR HOME AT ALL TIMES.

MY MARKETING PROCESS
"THE SECRET OF MY SUCCESS"

1. **COMPANY TOUR.** PERSONALLY CONDUCT A TOUR OF YOUR HOME FOR ALL THE SALES AGENTS IN MY OFFICE.
2. **THE MULTIPLE LISTING ASSOCIATION.** PROFESSIONALLY REPRESENT YOUR HOME TO THE MULTIPLE LISTING ASSOCIATION. AS A RESULT, YOUR HOME WILL BE EXPOSED TO EVERY AGENT IN YOUR AREA.
3. **BROKERS OPEN HOUSES.** HOLD BROKERS OPEN HOUSES FOR AGENTS IN THE MULTIPLE UNTIL THE PROPERTY HAS SOLD. I SHINE IN THIS AREA!

1

© 1986 Barb Schwarz

4. **FLYERS.** PROFESSIONALLY CREATE, PRODUCE, AND SEND AT LEAST ONE FLYER ABOUT YOUR HOME TO EACH AND EVERY AGENT IN THE MULTIPLE LISTING ASSOCIATION. AGENTS WATCH FOR MY FLYERS.

5. **EXCLUSIVE MAILING LIST.** PREPARE AND SEND A NEWSLETTER ABOUT YOUR HOME TO MY OWN EXCLUSIVE MAILING LIST OF THE TOP SELLING AGENTS IN THE MULTIPLE. THIS HAS BEEN AN EXTREMELY EFFECTIVE MARKETING TOOL AS AGENTS WATCH FOR MY LETTERS!

6. **AGENT RAPPORT.** I STRIVE TO MOTIVATE AGENTS TO SHOW AND SELL YOUR HOME THROUGH MY MANY PERSONAL CONTACTS. I HAVE ESTABLISHED AND CONSTANTLY WORK TO MAINTAIN A HIGH RAPPORT WITH THE WORKING AGENTS IN THE MULTIPLE.

7. **ADVERTISING.** OUR COMPANY MAINTAINS ONE OF THE MOST EXTENSIVE ADVERTISING PROGRAMS IN THE AREA. ADVERTISEMENTS FOR YOUR HOME WILL BE PLACED IN THE LOCAL MEDIA ON A REGULAR BASIS.

8. **PUBLIC OPEN HOUSES.** HOLD PUBLIC OPEN HOUSES ACCORDING TO YOUR WISHES.

MY COMMUNICATION WITH YOU

1. AS WE BEGIN OUR SELLER/AGENT RELATIONSHIP I GIVE YOU MY PERSONAL COMMITMENT THROUGH HOURS OF DIRECT COMMUNICATION REGARDING THE CURRENT MARKET AND THE MARKETING OF YOUR HOME.

2. I WILL VERBALLY KEEP IN TOUCH WITH YOU AT LEAST ONCE A WEEK AS MY WORK PROGRESSES FOR YOU.

3. I WILL PROVIDE A WRITTEN REPORT EVERY 4-6 WEEKS TO FULLY INFORM YOU OF ALL MY WORK AND THE MARKETING DONE ON YOUR BEHALF TO THAT DATE.

THE SALE

1. BE PRESENT, WHEN CONTACTED, AT ANY AND ALL EARNEST MONEY AGREEMENT PRESENTATIONS.

2. QUALIFY ALL PURCHASERS TO THE BEST OF MY ABILITY.

3. I KEEP ABREAST OF ALL CURRENT FINANCING PROGRAMS AVAILABLE. I WILL HELP THE PURCHASER FIND THE BEST FINANCING POSSIBLE TODAY.

CLOSING THE TRANSACTION

1. CONSTANTLY KEEP YOU INFORMED AS TO THE PROGRESS OF YOUR EARNEST MONEY AGREEMENT FROM THE TIME OF SIGNING UNTIL THE CLOSE OF YOUR SALE.

2. **ESCROW AND CLOSING.** I WORK HARD TO HANDLE ANY SITUATION THAT MAY ARISE WITH MORTGAGE BANKERS, ESCROW AGENTS, APPRAISERS, UNDERWRITERS, INSPECTORS, PURCHASERS, AND OTHER AGENTS DURING THE TIME OF ESCROW UP TO THE ACTUAL CLOSE OF YOUR SALE.

3. GO WITH YOU, IF YOU SO DESIRE, TO THE SIGNING OF YOUR CLOSING DOCUMENTS.

THE ABOVE MARKETING PROGRAM IS MY COMMITMENT TO YOU! I WILL WORK HARD TO REPRESENT YOU IN THE PROMPT SALE OF YOUR HOME AT THE BEST POSSIBLE PRICE. WHEN AND ONLY WHEN YOU HAVE RECEIVED THE PROCEEDS FROM THE SALE OF YOUR HOME DO I RECEIVE PAYMENT FOR MY SERVICES.

I LOOK FORWARD TO SERVING YOU!

SINCERELY,

3

Barb's Marketing Update Report

For

It is my sincere pleasure to be representing you as your listing and marketing agent in the sale of your home. Below is listed some of the work that I have completed to date for you, as we work together towards a successful completion of our goal.

(Your report by date goes here)

Samples i.e.

June 10th — Held Broker's Open from 10:00 to 1:00. I served refreshments to the agents. Comments were good with 18 agents attending.

June 14th — An ad was run in The Seattle Times in the Open House section for Sunday. I held open house from 2:00 to 5:00 P.M. and had a low turn-out. There was one couple looking in a lower price range and a single person looking for decorating ideas.

June 18 — Worked on a creative flyer for 3 hours in the afternoon promoting your home. This will be published and distributed to 2,000 agents next week in our multiple.

I hope you are pleased with the above work that I have completed to this date for you. I shall continue my work and dedication as we progress towards a completed sale of your home. Thank you.

Most sincerely,

(Your Name)
(Your Title)
(Your Company)

THE (Seller's Name) RESIDENCE

OFFERED AT $

ADDRESS:
AREA:
AGE:
STYLE:
SQUARE FOOTAGE:
BEDROOMS:
BATHS:
BASEMENT:
GARAGE:
LOT SIZE:
PROPERTY TAXES:
TERMS:
LENDER INFORMATION:

UNIQUE FEATURES:

SELLER'S REQUEST FOR
VERIFICATION OF LOAN INFORMATION

Requested of:

Lender _____

Address _____

_____

RE:

Loan Number _____

Property Address _____

_____

Dear Lender:

Please provide the following information to our agent:

Name _____

Company _____

Address _____

City _____ State _____ Zip _____

Type of Loan: _____ Original Amount $ _____ Interest Rate _____

Origination Date: _____ Present Balance $ _____

Original Term: _____ Prepayment Penalty, if any _____

Has Loan Been Sold? _____ To Whom? _____

Address _____

Payment Information: Assumption Information:

Principal and Interest $ _____ Is Loan Assumable? Yes ____ No ____

Reserve for Taxes $ _____ Assumption Fee? (Amount) _____

Reserve for Insurance $ _____ Credit Package Required? _____

Reserve for M.I.P. $ _____ Interest Rate to Remain Same? _____

Other _____ Adjusted Rate, if Applicable _____

Total Monthly Payments $ _____

Lender's requirements if property is sold, subject to existing loan, on a:

Real Estate Contract? _____

Note and Deed of Trust? _____

Sincerely,

_____ (owner) by _____

Authorized Signature of Lender

_____   Title/Position: _____

Name

_____   Telephone Number: _____

Address

_____   Date: _____

City _____ State _____ Zip

Steps To Make Your Loan Application Easier

To speed up the process of making your mortgage loan application please make sure you have all of the following information. Incomplete information will delay the process and could even delay your purchase. Please compile the following:

1.   A copy of the Sales Contract on the home that you're buying.

2.   A check for $_____, payable to the mortgage company for your credit report and/or appraisal fee. When the loan is approved, this is credited toward your closing costs. If for some reason the loan is not approved or the house does not appraise, this money will *not* be refunded to you.

3.   Social Security numbers for husband and wife, or each purchaser.

4.   Savings account numbers, addresses, and balances. Gift letter for any monies received from relatives to purchase home and placed in checking/savings account.

5.   Mutual Fund account numbers, addresses, and balances.

6.   Serial numbers and face values of any U.S. Savings Bonds and other stocks.

7.   A list of account numbers for all checking, savings, and credit union accounts. Please have the current balance of each account as well as the complete address.

8.   Credit card account numbers, balances, and monthly payments.

9.   A list of any debts you have. Include the name of the creditor, address, telephone number, account number, the monthly payment, and current balance.

10.   A list of assets, including insurance policies (cash value), cars, and furniture (and an estimate of their value).

11.   Name(s) and address(s) of employer(s) for the last five years. Latest earnings statement or pay vouchers.

12. If overtime is a substantial part of gross income, provide W-2 forms for the last three years. Commission sales usually require three years' W-2s.

13. If you are self-employed, tax returns for yourself and your business for the last two or three years will be required, plus profit and loss statements and balance sheets.

14. If you are getting a Veterans Administration loan, your certificate of eligibility if you have one or a Statement of Service or Discharge Papers if you don't.

15. Name and account number of Credit Union and balance.

16. If you presently own or have owned a home in the last three years, the name and address of the mortgage company or lending institution, the loan number, and balance.

17. If you are obtaining your equity from the sale of your previous residence, a copy of your closing statement is required.

18. If you are a landlord, bring a copy of your tenant's lease with you to substantiate income derived. (If no lease is available, bring copies of checks, receipts, etc.)

19. Any divorce papers and property settlements where property was involved in a divorce. If alimony or child support is being used as income to qualify for a loan, provide proof of amounts received.

20. If you or your co-applicant are receiving or are obliged to pay alimony, child support, or separate maintenance, bring a copy of your divorce decree and/or agreement.

21. Information on any retirement benefits which you or your company have. Provide addresses and account numbers. Also include all IRA and/or Keogh data.

22. Any bankruptcy judgment papers.

If you need further explanation or have questions about your unique circumstances, please contact me, your Realtor®, or your lender's representative. Being *totally* open and honest about all of your credit history is the best way to help you secure your mortgage in the quickest amount of time.

GLOSSARY OF FINANCING TERMS

ADJUSTABLE RATE MORTGAGE (ARM): A mortgage with an interest rate fixed for only a short period. At the end of the period the rate will be adjusted up or down based on current interest rate indexes.

AMORTIZED LOAN: A loan which is paid off in equal installments during its term.

ASSUMABLE MORTGAGE: A mortgage that can be transferred to a new owner. The new owner then assumes responsibility as the guarantor for the unpaid balance of the mortgage.

BALLOON PAYMENT: The final payment of a mortgage loan when it is larger than the regular payment. It usually extinguishes the debt.

CAPITAL GAINS TAX: The tax on profit derived from the sale of a capital asset. The capital gain is the difference between the sale price and the basis of the property, after making appropriate adjustments for closing costs, fixing up expenses, capital improvements, allowable depreciation, etc.

CLOSING COSTS: Expenses incurred in the closing of a real estate or mortgage transaction. Purchasers expenses normally include: cost of title examination, premiums for the title policies, credit report, appraisal fees, attorney fee, lender's service fees and recording charges.

CONVENTIONAL MORTGAGE: A loan neither FHA insured nor guaranteed by the VA. A loan approved under Fannie Mae or Freddiemac guidelines.

EQUITY: The difference between market value of the property and the owner's indebtedness.

ESCROW PAYMENT: A portion of a mortgagor's monthly payment held in trust by the lender to pay for taxes, insurance, mortgage insurance, and other items that become due.

FHA: The Federal Housing Administration. Sets guidelines for special lower interest loans on lower priced homes.

FANNIE MAE: Nickname for Federal National Mortgage Association (FNMA), a tax-paying corporation created by Congress. Sets guidelines under which most conventional mortgages are acceptable. FNMA is the largest purchaser of VA, FHA, and Conventional loans. Since FNMA buys so many loans from lenders, most loans must conform to their guidelines.

FREDDIEMAC: Nickname of Federal Home Loan Mortgage Corporation (FHLMC), a federally controlled and operated corporation to support the secondary mortgage market. It purchases and sells residential conventional home mortgages.

LOAN COMMITMENT: A written promise by a lender to make a loan under certain terms and conditions. These include interest rate, length of the loan, lender fees, annual percentage rate, mortgage and hazard insurance, and other special requirements.

LOAN TO VALUE RATIO: The ratio of the mortgage loan principal (amount borrowed) to the property's appraised value (selling price). On a $100,000 home, with a mortgage loan principal of $80,000, the loan to value ratio is 80%.

ORIGINATION FEE: A fee or charge for work involved in the evaluation, preparation, and submission of a proposed mortgage loan.

POINT: One percent of loan amount. Loan fees are sometimes expressed in points.

PREPAYMENT PENALTY: A fee paid to the mortgagee for paying the mortgage before it becomes due. Also known as prepayment fee or reinvestment fee.

PREPAYMENT PRIVILEGE: The right given a purchaser to pay all or part of a debt prior to its maturity without penalty.

PRIVATE MORTGAGE INSURANCE (PMI): Insurance written by a private company protecting the mortgage lender against loss occasioned by a mortgage default.

SECOND MORTGAGE: An additional loan on a property that becomes second in position behind the first mortgage. Generally at a higher interest rate and shorter terms than a first mortgage.

TITLE: Often used interchangeably with the word ownership. It indicates the accumulation of all rights in a property.

TITLE INSURANCE: An insurance policy which protects the insured (purchaser or lender) against loss arising from defects in title.

VA: Veterans Administration loans are available to all qualified veterans. In general, the veterans must have served more than 180 days continuous active duty and received an honorable discharge. The VA requires no downpayment and offers higher loan limits than FHA.

YOUR PERSONAL MOVING CHECK LIST

SIX WEEKS BEFORE MOVING:

Make an inventory of everything to be moved

Collect everything not to be moved for garage sale or charity

Contact charity for date/time of pickup. Save receipts for tax records

Contact several moving companies for estimates

Select mover, arrange for exact form of payment at destination (cash, check). Get cartons and packing materials to start packing NOW

Contact insurance agent to transfer or cancel coverage

Check with employer to find out what moving expenses they will pay

FOUR WEEKS BEFORE MOVING:

Notify all magazines of change of address

Check with veterinarian for pet records and immunizations

Contact utility companies for refunds of deposit; set turn-off dates

Dry clean clothes to be moved; pack in protective wrappers

Collect everything you have loaned out; return everything you have borrowed

Service power mowers, boats, snowmobiles, etc., that are to be moved. Drain all gas/oil to prevent fire in moving van

Check with doctors and dentist for all family records and prescriptions

Get childrens' school records

Check freezer and plan use of food over next 2-3 weeks

Remove all jewelry and other valuables to a safe deposit box or other safe place to prevent loss during move

Give away or arrange for transportation of house plants (most moving companies will NOT move plants, especially in winter). Plants also can be sold at garage sales, or are perfect "thank you" gifts for neighbors

ONE WEEK BEFORE MOVING:

Transfer or close checking and savings accounts. Arrange for cashiers check or money order to pay moving company upon arrival in new community

Have automobile serviced for trip

Fill out Post Office change of address forms; give to postmaster

Check and make inventory of all furniture for dents and scratches; notify moving company of your inventory and compare on final day

Dispose of all combustibles and spray cans (spray cans can explode or burn - don't pack them)

Pack a separate carton of cleaning utensils and tools (screw driver, hammer, etc.)

Separate cartons and luggage you need for personal/family travel

Mark all boxes that you pack with the room they will be going to in new home

Organize at least one room in the house for packers and movers to work freely

Cancel all newspapers, garden service, etc.

Review the entire list to make certain that you haven't overlooked anything

Check and double check everything you have done before it's too late

---

MOVING DAY:

Plan to spend the entire day at the house. Last minute decisions must be made by you. Don't leave until after the movers have gone

Hire a baby-sitter or send the children to a friend's house for the day

Stay with the moving van driver to oversee inventory

Tell packers and/or driver about fragile or precious items

Make a final check of the entire house, basement, closets, shelves, attic, garage, every room

Approve and sign the Bill of Lading. If possible, accompany driver to weigh station

Double check with the driver to make certain moving company records show the proper delivery address for your new house. Verify the scheduled delivery date as well.

Give driver phone numbers both here and in new community to contact you in case of a problem

Get complete routing information from the driver and phone numbers so you can call the driver or company in case of emergency while enroute

Disconnect all utilities and advise the Realtor® who sold or is selling your house

Lock all the doors and windows. Advise your Realtor® and neighbors that the house is empty

Moving does take lots of time and energy, and can be a stressful experience for some people. Use this list. It will definitely help. There is no substitute for good planning. Plan ahead! "Roll with the punches" and things will go more smoothly. Try to relax and enjoy the adventure.

AMORTIZATION CHART

To Compute Monthly Payment per $1,000

Interest Rate	5 Yrs	10 Yrs	15 Yrs	20 Yrs	25 Yrs	30 Yrs
7.00%	19.80	11.61	9.03	7.78	7.15	6.73
7.25%	19.92	11.74	9.16	7.92	7.29	6.88
7.50%	20.04	11.87	9.29	8.06	7.43	7.03
7.75%	20.16	12.00	9.42	8.21	7.57	7.18
8.00%	20.28	12.13	9.56	8.36	7.72	7.34
8.25%	20.40	12.27	9.70	8.52	7.88	7.51
8.50%	20.52	12.40	9.85	8.68	8.05	7.69
8.75%	20.64	12.53	9.99	8.84	8.22	7.87
9.00%	20.76	12.67	10.14	9.00	8.39	8.05
9.25%	20.88	12.80	10.29	9.16	8.56	8.23
9.50%	21.00	12.94	10.44	9.32	8.74	8.41
9.75%	21.12	13.08	10.59	9.49	8.91	8.59
10.00%	21.25	13.22	10.75	9.65	9.09	8.78
10.25%	21.37	13.35	10.90	9.82	9.26	8.96
10.50%	21.49	13.49	11.05	9.98	9.44	9.15
10.75%	21.62	13.63	11.21	10.15	9.62	9.33
11.00%	21.74	13.78	11.37	10.32	9.80	9.52
11.25%	21.87	13.92	11.52	10.49	9.98	9.71
11.50%	21.99	14.06	11.68	10.66	10.16	9.90
11.75%	22.12	14.20	11.84	10.84	10.35	10.09
12.00%	22.24	14.35	12.00	11.01	10.53	10.29
12.25%	22.37	14.49	12.16	11.19	10.72	10.48
12.50%	22.50	14.64	12.33	11.36	10.90	10.67
12.75%	22.63	14.78	12.49	11.54	11.09	10.87
13.00%	22.75	14.93	12.65	11.72	11.28	11.06
13.25%	22.88	15.08	12.82	11.89	11.47	11.26
13.50%	23.01	15.23	12.98	12.07	11.66	11.45
13.75%	23.14	15.38	13.15	12.25	11.85	11.75
14.00%	23.27	15.53	13.32	12.44	12.04	11.85

FOR EXAMPLE:
The payment on a $125,000 loan at 9 1/2% for 30 years would be $1051.25 per month ($8.41 X 125).

ESTIMATE OF PURCHASER'S EXPENSES

Prepared for: _____

Prepared by: _____ Date: _____

Property Address: _____

Based on sales price of: $_____   Loan Amount: $_____

                Real Estate Taxes............................$_____

                Hazard Insurance...........................$_____

                Mortgage Insurance.......................$_____

                Mortgagee Title Insurance..............$_____

                Loan Service Fee (%)................$_____

                Document Recording.....................$_____

                Appraisal Fee................................$_____

                Escrow or Closing Agent................$_____

                Credit Report................................$_____

                Tax Registration Fee.......................$_____

                Inspections...................................$_____

                Miscellaneous...............................$_____

                      SUBTOTAL.................................$_____

         Down Payment...................................$_____

                     TOTAL...$_____

Please Note: These figures are good faith estimates based on our experience and reflect current rates and charges. Actual expenses will be calculated by a closing officer and will vary with the specifics of the final sales transaction.

Barb
INCORPORATED

BARB SCHWARZ, CSP'

Dear Valued Client:

In our rapidly changing world choosing a real estate agent whom
you like and trust, to represent and market your most valuable
possession is a difficult decision.

My name is Barb Schwarz, a Realtor® with Barb Incorporated. I'd
like to introduce you to my abilities, my accomplishments, and my
interests via the Career Book® you now hold in your hands.

When choosing a real estate agent, you as the homeowner become an
employer. You have the right to know the credentials and the
expertise of the agent you hire to market your home. I believe
strongly in making this information available to you and welcome
the opportunity to leave my Career Book® with you. It is not
just a portfolio of my personal and business successes; it also
contains valuable information on many different aspects of real
estate in today's market.

Please take your time, enjoy this guided tour through my career,
and I will return for it at our agreed-upon time. It's then that
I will be happy to answer any questions that have occurred to you
and further discuss the strategies I will use to effectively
market your home or help you find the home of your choice.

Sincerely,

Barb Schwarz, CSP
Barb Incorporated

BARB SCHWARZ CSP'
1224 212th Avenue S f • Issaquah WA 98027
(800) 392-7161 • (206) 391-2072 • Fax 206-391-5416
'CSP = the highest award in professional speaking presented by the National Speakers Association

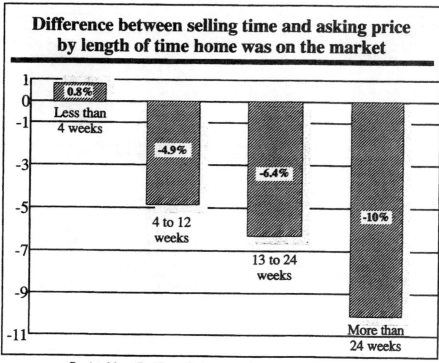

Difference between selling time and asking price by length of time home was on the market

1
0   **0.8%**
-1   Less than
     4 weeks
-3   **-4.9%**
                  -6.4%
-5   4 to 12   **-10%**
     weeks
-7   13 to 24
            weeks
-9
-11   More than
                           24 weeks

Reprinted from "Real Estate Outlook" © National Association of Realtors®

TODAY

I'm going to help someone today.

Someone needs my help to sell a home ... not just a house.
Chances are they've
> *Lived there...*
>> *Loved there...*
and despite the faults of the house or the owners, it's a home.
To them, I pledge the respect that I would want others to have
for my home and for the members of my family.

Someone needs my help today to find a home ...
not just a house. Invariably a new home means new hope for
> *a new opportunity*
> *a new job*
> *a new marriage*
> *... or a new start*
> *a new neighborhood*
> *a new chance*
for the warmth and joy and friends and fulfillment they picture
for themselves in their very best moments.

Not many people get the opportunity to help people
in times so dear to life
> *... but I do*
> *and I can*
> *and I will*
> *for their sake*
> *and for mine.*

Author Unknown

It's unwise to pay too much...
but it's worse to pay too little.
When you pay too much, you lose
a little money...and that is all.
When you pay too little,
you sometimes lose everything,
because the thing you bought was incapable
of doing the thing it was bought to do.
The common law of business balance
prohibits paying a little and getting a lot...
it can't be done.
If you deal with the lowest bidder,
it is well to add something for the risk you run.
And if you do that,
you will have enough
to pay for something better.

John Ruskin

You do what you *are*.
You are what you *think*.
And what you think is determined
by what you *learn*.
What you learn is determined
by what you *experience*.
What you experience is determined
by what you *expose yourself to*.
And what you expose yourself to
is determined by what you *do*.
What you do is determined
by what you *are* and what your destiny is.

Barb Schwarz